COOKING *for the* GODS

Painted Pot Lid

Catalogue no. 57

COOKING for the GODS

The Art of Home Ritual in Bengal

catalogue by

Pika Ghosh

with essays by

Edward C. Dimock

Pika Ghosh

Lee Horne

Michael W. Meister

edited by

Michael W. Meister

The Newark Museum

This publication presents a significant component of the Newark Museum's permanent South Asian collection. It was first published in conjunction with an exhibition, *Cooking for the Gods: The Art of Home Ritual in Bengal,* organized by The Newark Museum and the University of Pennsylvania History of Art Department, and on view at The Newark Museum from October 1995 through June 1996.

The exhibition and catalogue were funded by the National Endowment for the Arts, the Geraldine R. Dodge Foundation Inc., the New Jersey Council for the Humanities, the New Jersey State Council on the Arts/Department of State, the History of Art Department's Museum Studies Fund, and Dr. David R. Nalin and the Merck Company Foundation.

NEW JERSEY
STATE
COUNCIL
ON THE
ARTS

The Newark Museum receives operating support from the City of Newark and the State of New Jersey, The New Jersey State Council of the Arts/Department of State, and Essex County. Funding for acquisitions and activities other than operations must be developed from outside sources.

Library of Congress Cataloging-in-Publication Data

Cooking for the Gods : the art of home ritual in Bengal / catalogued
   by Pika Ghosh ; with essays by Edward C. Dimock . . . [et al.] ;
   edited by Michael W. Meister.
       p.   cm.
     Includes bibliographical references.
     ISBN 0-932828-32-9
     1. Hinduism—Liturgical objects—Exhibitions. 2. Cookery—
Religious aspects—Hinduism—Exhibitions. 3. Hinduism—India—
Bengal—Customs and practices—Exhibitions. 4. Bengal (India)—
Religious life and customs—Exhibitions. I. Ghosh, Pika, 1969–.
II. Dimock, Edward C.   III. Meister, Michael W.
BL1236.72.C66   1995   95-36877
294.5′37—dc20   CIP

Distributed by The University of Pennsylvania Press
423 Guardian Drive
Philadelphia, PA 19104
ISBN 0-8122-1589-3

Composition: G&S Typesetters
Printer: Cadmus Promotional Printing
Editor: Ingalill H. Hjelm
Designer: Adrianne Onderdonk Dudden

Printed in the United States of America

Foreword

The Newark Museum's presentation of *Cooking for the Gods: The Art of Home Ritual in Bengal* is the culmination of a ten-year process of assembling and researching an important collection of South Asian art. The Museum is greatly indebted to Dr. David R. Nalin and his family for their generosity in donating such a rich and diverse group of images, ritual objects, and implements from India and Bangladesh.

The Nalin Collection was given to the Museum in appreciation of its long-standing commitment to the contextual presentation of Asian art. As early as 1909, Museum founder John Cotton Dana sought to introduce Americans to world culture through educational exhibitions and publications. In the last decade, The Newark Museum has been recognized as a model for innovative exhibitions and programs to interpret Asian art, exemplified by the creation of a traditional Buddhist Altar using Tibetan artisans and advisers to showcase its renowned Tibetan collection.

This Bengali catalogue and the exhibition it accompanies were shaped through a collaboration between The Newark Museum and the University of Pennsylvania.

Guiding the project with great sensitivity and insight were Valrae Reynolds, Curator of Asian Collections at The Newark Museum, and Dr. Michael W. Meister, Professor and Chairman, Department of the History of Art, University of Pennsylvania. The History of Art Department's Museum Studies Fund allowed Pika Ghosh to research and catalogue the entire collection at the Museum in 1993, 1994, and 1995.

The Trustees of the Newark Museum are indebted to the National Endowment for the Arts, the Geraldine R. Dodge Foundation, Inc., the New Jersey Council for the Humanities, the New Jersey State Council on the Arts/Department of State, Dr. David R. Nalin, and the Merck Company Foundation for their crucial support of the exhibition and catalogue, which have enabled us to depict the full humanities content of these fascinating objects.

Mary Sue Sweeney Price
Director, The Newark Museum

Acknowledgments

This catalogue is the result of a happy conjunction of people who share a deep empathy for the art of the Indian subcontinent. Dr. David R. Nalin, while in India and Bangladesh from 1967 to 1980 doing medical research, collected the everyday as well as the ancient artifacts of the regions where he was stationed. His interest in The Newark Museum began when he was headquartered in New Jersey in the 1980s. Dr. Nalin became a friend of the Museum just as it was embarking on a major expansion and renovation. Newark's Asian collections, so rich in Far Eastern and Himalayan material, were lacking in just the sort of Indian art which Dr. Nalin had collected. Through the generosity of David R. Nalin as well as his brother Richard J. Nalin and other members of his family, over one thousand objects were donated to The Newark Museum between 1985 and 1994.

Once committed to the presentation of the Nalin collection of Bengali material, the Museum was fortunate to enlist the cooperation of Dr. Michael W. Meister, Professor and Chairman, Department of the History of Art, University of Pennsylvania, who enthusiastically supported the idea of a collaborative venture between the Museum and the University. It was not until Pika Ghosh came to the University as a beginning graduate student, however, that the themes of domestic ritual and womens' empowerment crystallized. Ms. Ghosh grew up in Calcutta surrounded by just such objects of worship in everyday life. She was thus able to bring an insider's viewpoint as well as to examine the collection with an art historian's eye.

Ms. Ghosh's essay, *Household Rituals and Women's Domains,* conveys the rich context in which these images and utensils are used in Bengali tradition. Dr. Meister has overseen all of the catalogue organization as well as contributed an essay on *Categories of Utility* which investigates the interrelations of art and artifact and of form and use.

We have also been fortunate to have contributions from Edward C. Dimock and Lee Horne. In *Bhakti,* Dr. Dimock discusses the many levels of meaning in the offering of food and the devotional relationships between humans and gods in Bengal. Dr. Horne's *Making Metal in West Bengal,* explains the complex history and social context of metal craftsmen serving the Bengal cultural area. Together, these individuals have given The Newark Museum the opportunity to show a broad audience the intimate relationship between art and life in Hindu Bengal.

Valrae Reynolds
Curator of Asian Collections

Collector's Preface

My earliest recollections of collecting folk images from Bengal are those of domestic nuisance—the stubborn refusal of itinerant brass-wallahs to quit my doorstep in Dhaka, Bangladesh, without showing their wares. My only ticket to restored peace and privacy was, unavoidably, the spilling of miscellaneous metal objects from bulging grimy jute gunny sacks onto my living room carpet.

Gazing over objects salvaged from the metal recycling shops of Old Dhaka, harvested by metal scavengers who combed remote villages for broken pots and worn images of gods and goddesses traded by needy housewives, a bicycle part here, an old jewelry mold there, a brass Krishna or a fragment of a Pala bronze, all lay unappreciated before me, until one day during a visit to New York, I noticed similar objects (less the bicycle part) on display at an Asia Society exhibition, and began to collect them.

Ultimately this collection included among its folk images many examples from Bengal, encompassing Hindu, Buddhist, and tribal images, one of the largest groups of sixteenth- to twentieth-century Krishna-Radha sculptures of the *bhakti* cult, *dhokra* metal work, and Dhaka painted plates echoing the palette and linear outlines of early Pala palm-leaf paintings and of the twentieth-century Kalighat School. Examples were added of sculpture in metal, wood, terracotta, and porcelain, and of painted and woven images.

Though later entranced by the exquisite studies in formality of Pala-Sena sculptures in the high tradition, some examples of which are included here, I often found myself drawn back to the immediacy and ingenuous charm and humor of devotional folk images, and to the wholly satisfying formal integrity of the vessels used in their worship: pots to be filled with holy Gangetic water or with milk offerings for serpents, braziers, and censers to be filled with coals and smoking camphor tablets swung by dancers before the goddess during *puja*, stands for black stone *shalagramas*, brass platters with mirrorlike polish for offerings of Bengali sweets, incense holders, bells with *garuda* handles, a cornucopia of vibrant forms, and simple bowls which, when struck, hum with a resonance evoking another era and another reality.

Primitive workmanship (as in the *Durga*, no. 3) and the recycling of ancient motifs infuse archaistic elements into some of the modern images and vessels. The twentieth-century bird-faced terracotta mother goddess figurines (nos. 64–66) recall mother goddess images of the first to third centuries B.C. Other images, however straightforward and brash in contrast to the subtle *déhanchements* of Bengal Pala sculptures, retain remarkably faithful adherence to iconographic detail (no. 4).

The concentrated ritual power of some of the objects reflects the primitive opaqueness of the godhead to man, recognizable in the abstract worship of numinous village hallows, where rocks or twisted roots of ancient trees are daubed with crimson and yellow paste. Still others incorporate new forms, such as the automobile-shaped *pan* box (no. 42), the ultimate modern vehicle (*vahana*), perhaps the Model T *garuda* fit for the viceregal brass images of *Vishnu* and his consort (no. 18).

The mythic wishing trees and lions, bulls, elephants, and leogryphs rampant or leaping from wondrous vines, proliferative life forms, and decorative floral motifs, peacocks and parrots, fish and scorpions on offering stands, incense holders, bowls, and metal shrines, recall *prana*, the creative fullness of life force. The strength of the aspect of divine manifestation in domestic worship left its most lasting impression on me when my Bengali teacher and friend, Ananta Kumar Chakraborty, told me how his grandfather had developed such intense powers of concentrated meditation that he could bring the goddess into the palm of his hand—a religious experience perhaps echoed in the tradition of miniature images of *devas* and *devis* represented in the collection.

The gift of more than one thousand works to The Newark Museum was made in the hope that these once venerated images and the vessels used in their worship could be in a sense reborn, as *avatars* to the New World. The present exhibition and catalogue have begun to make this hope a reality by displaying selected objects, like flowers from the stems and roots of ancient traditions, in their cultural and religious context. For this I thank especially Pika Ghosh, Valrae Reynolds, and Michael W. Meister, as well as the other distinguished contributors to the catalogue and the exhibition.

Dr. David R. Nalin

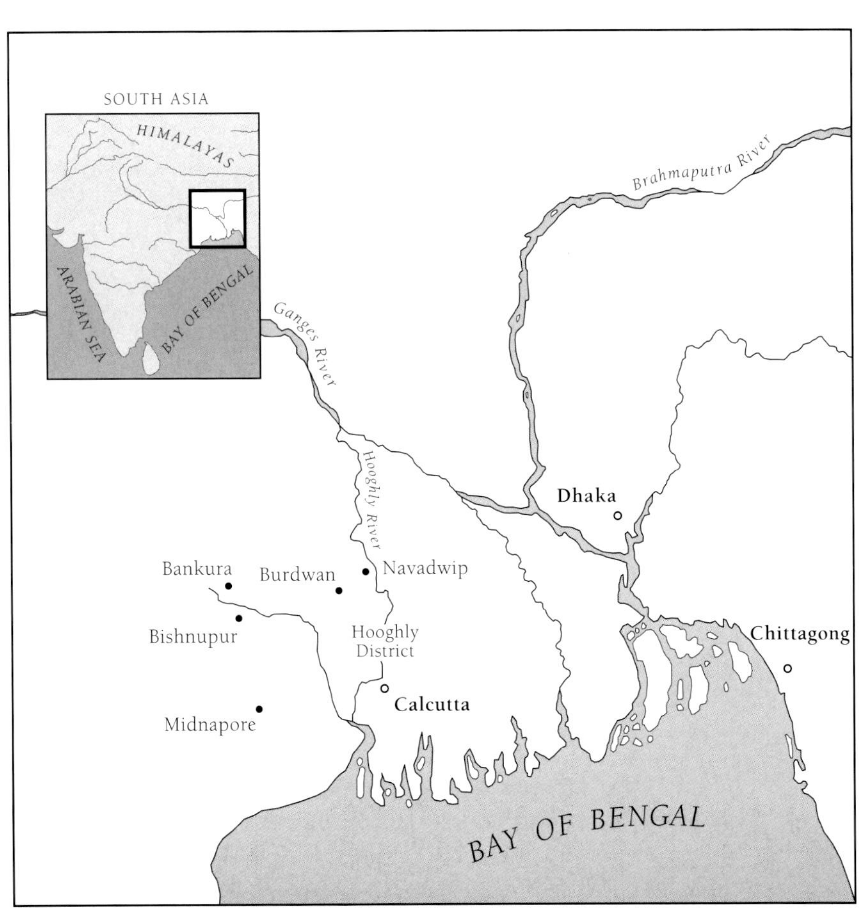

Bengali Cultural Region

Contents

A woman sets out sweets on a bell-metal plate.

Women offer food after it has been blessed by the gods at the altar.

Introduction

PIKA GHOSH

Through a range of household objects from cutting knives to exquisitely carved shrines, this exhibition will bring before a wide audience the close relationship between ritual and daily life in the eastern Indian region known as Bengal. The women who cook meals for the family in the home also prepare food for the gods and goddesses of the household shrines. Deities step out of their shrines to preside not only over the household altar but also over the kitchen fire. Objects of the sort used to cook dinner for the family are also used to serve the deities their meals. The food, having first been offered to the gods, is consumed by the family as a palpable piece of divine grace and the blessings of the gods are internalized by eating the leftovers from the gods' meal (*prasada*).

Cooking is one of the ritual acts that articulates the relationship between the worshiper and the gods in Bengali homes. The words, gestures, actions and objects used to maintain this relationship may be expressed collectively by the term *puja*.[1] A useful definition for *puja* in the Bengali context can be extracted from Akos Ostor's work on the subdivisional town of Bishnupur in West Bengal:

> Puja means honor or respect, an act of offering something to someone. . . . *Puja* is expressive as concept, act, and relationship. It symbolizes in word and deed the very beliefs and actions that constitute the sacred in Bengal.[2]

The relationship between the gods and their devotees is at the core of domestic worship. The gods who reside in the home shrine and consume the cooked offerings are numerous, and quite distinctive in their personalities, powers, and eccentricities. They are chosen from a vast pantheon ranging from Brahmanical deities such as Krishna (no. 5) to deities with non-Sanskritic origins such as Manasa, the snake goddess.[3] Especially endearing aspects of a deity are chosen to be loved and adored within the home. Here women adopt a more familiar and personal relationship with the deity. Nadugopala, the form of the baby Krishna stealing sweetmeats, for example, is treated like a child of the family (no. 8). In addition to a family's chosen deity, numerous other gods and goddesses are honored at particular times and for specific occasions.

These deities are received within the home with all the hospitality, respect, and honor due to a visiting guest; through ritual their every demand is satisfied, their every whim indulged. Implements of household ritual in the Newark Museum's collection such as incense stick holders and camphor censers (nos. 22, 26), for example, reflect the worshipers' desire to provide the gods with their most valued fragrances; handbells (no. 24) and conch shells give the gods their preferred sounds. In turn, the appeased gods and goddesses impart grace that will protect the home and grant the wishes of the family.

Cooking for the gods and goddesses is an activity that requires specialized knowledge. An informed familiarity with the palates and predilections of the household deities is essential. This information is passed down from wives to daughters and daughters-in-law. Daily offerings invariably include sweetmeats and fruit, made to please the taste of the particular deity being served, while more elaborate meals are prepared for special occasions. Krishna as a baby loves coconut sweets (*nadu*), for example, and this baby god is specifically identified by his weakness for these sweetmeats when he is called Nadugopala, the boy Gopala who eats *nadu* (no. 8).

Represented in the Newark Museum's collection are a variety of utensils used to prepare these foods. Molds for creating attractive floral patterns on the surface of the sweetmeats, for instance, reflect the care that women take in presenting meals to the gods and ensuring their well-being (no. 38). Serving dishes are often personalized by the incision of auspicious patterns associated with the deity to whom the object is dedicated. The name of the deity may sometimes be carved on the bottom of the plate, bowl, or drinking glass.

Cooking for gods in the home is an activity that highlights the intimacy established between the divine world and humanity, as well as the particular familiarity Bengali women develop toward their personal choice of gods and goddesses. It is uniquely in the home that women can freely, spontaneously, and directly approach the gods without the mediation of a priest. Cooking can therefore be understood in part as an activity by which these women can empower themselves in their own sphere.

Ethnographic Context

Bengal represents a cultural region shared now by India and Bangladesh. Ethnographic information presented in this catalogue derives primarily from field experience in West Bengal, but the rituals described are closely related to domestic rituals of Hindu women in Bangladesh and the Bengali diasporas around the world where women have carried their gods with them and continued to sustain them with food offerings.

Objects in the Newark Museum's collection, primarily collected in the eastern regions of Bengal, reflect many different facets of the cultural history of the Bengal delta. Some clay figurines (nos. 64, 65) reflect a class of terracottas that Stella Kramrisch has categorized as "ageless."[4] Similar terracottas have been fired in India since the third millennium and continue to be created by village artisans as toys for children (nos. 68–72). Other objects in the

collection highlight important moments in the history of Bengal. A Manasa water-pot (no. 29) and copper images of Vishnu (no. 12) represent the Pala and Sena dynasties that ruled Bengal from approximately the mid-eighth to the early twelfth centuries. A porcelain image of the Hindu goddess Durga Mahishamardini, on the other hand, suggests contact with European means of manufacture and can be dated to the colonial period (no. 9). This contact seems even more obvious in a porcelain Krishna and Radha (no. 10). An automobile-shaped metal container (no. 42) also reflects a playful interaction with Europe, especially with the British East India Company.

A majority of the Newark collection consists of implements for worship and daily household utensils that have been popular in Bengal over the past century and continue to be made and used in homes today. It is difficult to date objects of daily use accurately because of the long period over which similar forms have been used. Woven reed mats in this collection represent one of the variety of crafts practiced at home (nos. 43–46). These mats are spread on the earthen floor of rural huts for guests when they are served meals as well as for worshipers at prayer. Bell-metal pots for home use often resemble those still molded in clay by village potters today (no. 31).

Some of these implements display particular features of the cultural geography of the region in their form, function, and material. It is the soil itself that is still the dominant source of prosperity in rural Bengal. The earth is anthropomorphized as Lakshmi, the goddess of wealth, and expressed as the flowering pot in ritual. Wet rice cultivation and the harvesting of the ripened grain is an activity of great significance. Rice measuring bowls and covers for rice storage pots, for example, are utensils sometimes transformed by orna-

ment and ritual into embodiments of the goddess of wealth for use in home shrines (nos. 39, 56–58). The arrival of the annual monsoon rains so essential for agriculture and for the household supply of water is another dominant concern in Bengal. Manasa water-pots, as in the Pala example presented in this exhibition, are at the center of a ritual celebration of the monsoon's rains, when snakes emerge from the dampened earth and rising rivers (no. 29).

The genealogies of many of these household objects are complex and layered. It is not easy to classify them into "high" or "low," or to label them as "tribal," "folk," "urban," or even "tourist." Implements that are created by low-caste craftsmen with tribal ancestry can become the center of rural as well as urban Hindu ritual. Bowls made by the Malhar of Dariapur, for example, are used daily by rural and urban women as measuring bowls for cooking rice (no. 39). During festivals, these rice-measuring bowls embody Lakshmi, the goddess of rice and prosperity in home shrines.

The folk crafts of Bengal, because of growing urban popularity, can become commercial ventures as "folk art." Terracotta figurines, for example, have become fashionable in urban living rooms and are now produced industrially to satisfy increasing demand (nos. 64–67). Changes in patronage patterns for these objects have often led to changes in their iconography (no. 67); changes in production techniques, in turn, may lead to shifts in stylistic features (nos. 9, 10).

International markets and state intervention have increasingly dictated the shapes and forms of, for example, *dokra* figurines. These were first produced primarily for a rural clientele (nos. 59–63) but are now often manufactured for state emporia, urban art collectors, or international folk museums.[5] In this exhibition, however, the circumstances of their ritual and domestic use will form the basis for discussion.

Women's household rituals construct not just a gendered identity for their practitioners, but their reception may be a reflection of conflicts in Bengali society as a whole. As younger women begin to question the meaning of certain inherited household ritual activities and, on occasion, to reject them, they may insist on significant reorientations in their roles as wives and mothers. Yet in home rituals, these women still strengthen their identities as Bengalis and often bring such rituals into increasingly urban and Westernized environments.

Objects in "Art" Contexts

This exhibition draws from several strands of scholarship about art and cultural production. It is intended to examine some of the complexities in the relationships between "art" and the instruments of ritual in Bengal. A number of exhibitions in the past decade have attempted to place utilitarian objects of Indian origin within their particular cultural context[6] and avenues of academic interest have also opened that encourage greater discussion of domestic rituals and women's activities.[7] Those studying the religious practices of South Asia have also begun to shift much more of their attention from texts to performance. Nonwritten and even nonverbal genres of activity are invading the privileged territory of written texts.[8] This makes the material objects used to activate such ritual performances as collected here of increasing significance.

The ritual activities that orient the lives of Bengali women have rarely been explored in an exhibition, and objects specific to the Bengali domestic context have only occasionally been on museum dis-

play.[9] If this exhibition is intended to explore the intimate connection between ritual and domestic life in Bengal, however, it also requires that we redefine how "art" and "utility" function in the context of ritual use.

NOTES

1. See also Wendy Doniger, "The Role of Myth in the Indian Life Cycle," in *Aditi: The Living Arts of India* (Washington DC: The Smithsonian Institution, 1986), p. 185.
She describes this relationship with the divine:
. . . not only are the gods close to us in their nature; they are physically close to us in India, present on earth in incarnations or in disguised forms. Hindus feel intimate with their gods, able to address them and to offer them not only awestruck worship but small creature comforts: they feed their gods (as these appear in the form of metal or stone images in houses and temples), and then distribute the leftovers to the devotees as *prasada* or blessed food. They change their clothes, and fan them in the hot weather, and swing them on swings, and scratch their backs with specially sanctified back-scratchers. As evidence of the fact that the gods are so like us and come so much among us that it is hard to tell whether one is in the presence of a human or a god, certain texts offer five ways in which one may tell by looking at someone whether he or she is mortal or immortal: the gods never blink or sweat; their garlands never wither nor do their clothes become dusty; and their feet never quite touch the ground, but hover slightly above it.
2. Akos Ostor, *Puja in Society* (Lucknow: Ethnic and Folk Culture Society, 1982), p. 7.
3. Manasa probably has her origins in non-Brahmanical snake cults and was later incorporated into the fold of Brahmanical worship as an aspect of the great Goddess.
4. Stella Kramrisch, "Indian Terracottas," in *Exploring India's Sacred Art: Selected Writings of Stella Kramrisch,* edited by Barbara Stoler Miller (Philadelphia: University of Pennsylvania Press, 1983), p. 69.
5. Katherine F. Hacker, "Continuities and Transformations Among Living Sculptural Traditions: Wax-Thread Metal Images of Eastern India" (University of Pennsylvania, unpublished Ph.D. diss., 1993), pp. 14–30.
6. A notable example is Jyotindra Jain, ed., *Utensils* (Ahmedabad: The Gujarat Handicrafts Development Corporation and VECHAAR, 1990) which attempted to situate kitchen tools such as bell-metal water-pots and nutcrackers in the context of the Gujarati household. Two recent German exhibitions have explored the tribal rituals practiced by various groups in central India that had formed the traditional setting for a variety of ritual metal objects: A. L. Dallapiccola, *The Sacred and the Profane: Bell Metal Casting in the Folk Art of India* (Heidelberg: Völkerkundmuseum der von-Portheim-Stiftung, 1984); Cornelia Mallebrein, "Die Anderen Götter Volks- und Stammesbronzen aus Indien," in *Ethnologica* 17, 1993).
7. Two examples of such scholarship concerning Bengal are: Lina Fruzzetti, *The Gift of a Virgin: Women, Marriage and Ritual in a Bengali Society* (New Brunswick, NJ: Rutgers University Press, 1982) and Manisha Roy, *Bengali Women* (Chicago: University of Chicago Press, 1975).
8. Arjun Appadurai, "Introduction," in *Gender, Genre and Power in South Asian Expressive Traditions,* edited by Arjun Appadurai, Margaret Mills, and Frank Korom (Philadelphia: University of Pennsylvania Press, 1991), pp. 3–29.
9. *Mahamaya: The Crafts and Craftsmen of Eastern India* (The Crafts Council of West Bengal, 1986) and Robert Skelton and Mark Francis, *Arts of Bengal: The Heritage of Bangladesh and Eastern India* (London: Whitechapel Art Gallery, 1979).

A woman assists a priest by arranging food offerings around a shalagrama stone used for worship.

A priest and a woman arrange raw and cooked food for the worship of Vishnu.

Categories of Utility

MICHAEL W. MEISTER

It need not be surprising, in today's alleged-to-be post-modern, multicultural world, for *The New York Times* to report, under a now often used Sunday heading, "Arts/Artifacts," on the sale of Rudolf Nureyev's shoes, or for a review of *The Andy Warhol Museum* in the same paper to refer to the philosopher/critic Arthur Danto, whose essay for an exhibition entitled "ART/artifact" in 1988 may have provided a source for the *Times'* category.[1] In Danto's view,

> an artifact implies a system of means; to extract it from the system in which it has a function and display it for itself is to treat a means as though it were an end. The use of an artifact is its meaning.[2]

Art—a modern category for which many societies including those of ancient Greece and India had no separate word—Danto distinguishes by a different utility:

> an artwork is a compound of thought and matter. The material thing makes the thought. . . . An artifact is shaped by its function, but the shape of an artwork is given by its content.[3]

Herbert Muschamp's review in the same issue of *The New York Times* of an exhibition of Italian Renaissance architectural models at the National Gallery, Washington D.C., cites the formulation of a Marxist art historian of an earlier generation, Arnold Hausser, who described "the ascent of the artist from the level of the petit-bourgeois artisan to that of the free intellectual worker."[4] Yet it is the fine fringe between his role as "free intellectual worker" and as "artisan" that makes Warhol's "artifacts" art. To Oscar Wilde, at the end of the nineteenth century, "Art is the most intense mode of Individualism that the world has known; I am inclined to say that it is the only real mode of Individualism that the world has known."[5] He thus made man the artifact, his life the art.

Other times and places have had other categories. Today's conflicted dichotomies of high/low, arts/crafts, fine/decorative, folk/primitive—or the construction of newly minted groupings such as art/artifact—must be seen as both finely problematized and culturally defined.[6]

To understand this, we must recognize that the *use* of an object also materializes thought. In a special issue on "Art in Ritual Context" of the *Journal of Ritual Studies*, Richard Davis has pointed out that making an image *for* worship and its use *in* worship are each equally surrounded by rituals (what Danto might call a "system in which [the artifact] has a function"). In Davis's words, "there is never a time when the image exists as an unconsecrated object."[7] Yet in each stage of the object's use these sets of rituals may have separated meanings.

Both art and artifact refer to objects of man's making.[8] In a traditional context art often equals only those sets of rules that explain practice. The artifice of art is in its use. The thought in art both gives it form and makes it useful. Yet utility must be seen to transcend modern ideas limited to function. Form follows function in a ritual and traditional context as much on a level of symbolic understanding as one of material use.

A society such as India's provides a particular test for categories of utility as a measure of what is art. Danto found that

> for the Greeks, the artist revealed thought in the work of art, and the artist's passivity in regards to this was perhaps evidence of the *objective* truth of the thought that he expressed.[9]

A similar attitude toward the artist/artisan as a tool through which "truth" could be materialized also can be found in India's textual and oral traditions.[10] According to the great Indian art historian and curator, Stella Kramrisch,

> the arts and crafts in India partake in the nature of rites whose technical performance had magic power. . . . The range of the crafts extends over the entire culture and compromises the work of the wheelwright and the sculptor, or potter and perfumer, weaver and architect.[11]

Imbedded in the iconography of an object such as the fine seventeenth/eighteenth-century folk image of Durga as slayer of the buffalo demon that Dr. David R. Nalin has given to the Philadelphia Museum of Art as part of the Stella Kramrisch collection is a "system of thought" about the world, female energy, and the divine that governs the form similar images take over many centuries (nos. 3–4, 9, 57–58).

In her arms are weapons given her by male deities to strengthen her attack. To either side are Ganesha and Kartikeya, sons of Shiva. Behind her is an architectural frame. Here the vision of the goddess's implacable domination over the threatening demon is both visible and remembered; it moves from the eye quickly to the mind. On her arms are silver bracelets added over many years of worship as part of clothing offered by her devotees. The typology of such an object gives body to a mental image of the goddess; style, like a garment, only helps to bring it forward.

It is this power of such an icon to elicit a mental image that makes it beautiful to a worshiper. Our judgment of its rendering—the radiant frame of arms and the sinuous thrust of her long three-pronged spear—reflects rather than represents the power of that vision. To the devotee, the soft Europeanized esthetic of the nineteenth-century porcelain Durga in the Newark collection (no. 9), on the other hand, is much like the silver bracelets on this one—ornament only, a kind of clothing, acting as a stimulant to the memory.[12]

And yet, in the Nalin bronze, the intrusion of an individual artist's creative choice can also be seen. As Dr. Nalin perceptively has pointed out, the crown on the head of this image appropriates a European crown, perhaps first seen by the artisan on a coin or on an engraving brought to India by missionaries or representatives of the British East India Company. How fitting this appropriation is can be sensed by how nearly veiled it remains—one emblem of power poised unobtrusively above another—compared to the stylistic softness of nos. 9 and 10.

Ritual objects—art or implement—participate in action; they are part of a performance which they help to make material. Both viewers and actors participate through the objects used. These are, in part, the trace of that performance as a painting is a trace of its making. Yet thought and ritual, form and material are intertwined, inseparable. One implements the other in a ceaseless round of making and using, which, like Christo's wrapping, is not simply a "system of use" but mentality in action.

If a found object also can become art (no. 16), it does so through how it is received; that is, thought can also be separated from the form of an object and embodied in its use. Or perhaps we must say that it can be found in the nexus of form and use, as Duchamp's experiments with art as pure thought demand. "Art" is a category of reception, as in Danto's artful separation of objects with the same form that in one context are "thick with significations" and in an other simply implement "sustained utility."[13]

It is the combination of thought and utility that informs the objects in this exhibition. In the context of Bengali *bhakti*—the sustained emotional interaction of humanity, the physical world, and the divine —objects of use are objects of thought (no. 29). From the ritual spoon to the flame to the deity to the rituals of daily experience, the layers of perception and reception that modern Western thought has now begun to analyze are perceived as part of an "objectified truth" (in India, they form the recipe for its construction).[14]

The pot that cooks the rice can contain the deity (no. 31). The image that gives human form to a god is no less of an implement than the spoon (no. 18). A natural simile of ladle and vagina can express an identity that neither overpowers nor supplants the identity of each (no. 21). In a found stone can be seen the structure of the cosmos (no. 16). Through daily worship, we all become implements of that greatest artifice. And by sharing food with the deities we become an active part of what that ritual has implemented.

Davis describes the use of a South Indian metal image as a vessel to carry the deity from a temple's sanctum to worshipers outside of the temple during festivals:

> . . . during the daily processions Shiva's fullest presence would have been transferred into it, like coals being periodically kindled into flame, and it would have served them as a mobile icon of Shiva's grace, extending his favor beyond the restricted sphere of the inner sanctum.[15]

So too each of these implements carries the flame of thought, kindled periodically by both ritual and domestic use.

In India, an object's esthetic value is as much a consequence of its use and reception as of its making. As Western contemporary artists have begun again to reflect on the question of "what is art?" they have come up with answers that often are separated from the issue of beauty. Reporting on the appointment of a new chairman at the Museum of Modern Art, for example, *The New York Times* remarks that "contemporary artists are working on a much

An image of Durga Mahishamardini from Chitta-gong, made of copper with white-metal bracelets (late seventeenth/early eighteenth century; height: 7⅛″ width: 4½″) gifted by David R. Nalin to the Philadelphia Museum of Art (acc. no. 1985-18-1; courtesy Philadelphia Museum of Art).

larger scale than their predecessors, creating huge works and installations that require huge spaces"—perhaps partly a kind of anti-museum agenda to take art out once more into nature, life, and the world—thus leaving many pieces gifted to MOMA, such as a recent huge Richard Serra sculpture, "in museum storage in Brooklyn." David Rockefeller, chairman emeritus of the museum, is quoted as saying:

> So much contemporary art doesn't seem to place the aesthetic values on art that art should have. . . . That's a good reason I don't think I'm the right person to do the job.[16]

As in India, art in the West seems again to be struggling to extend its "favor beyond the restricted sphere of the inner sanctum."[17]

For this catalogue and exhibition, we have divided the objects from the Nalin collection in the Newark Museum into six categories and let them interlock in ways that emphasize their interchangeability. Home "shrines" form the first category—shelters intended to house images of the gods for home ritual (nos. 1, 2). Yet the shelter itself can be the object of worship, and the anthropomorphic "images" that form our second category are themselves conceived as vessels, inhabited, as are the shrines, only because of the rituals performed around them (nos. 3, 4). Whether "folk" (no. 11) or "fine art" (nos. 12, 13), nearly worn out or recently clothed (nos. 3, 4), these images are treated ritually in similar ways. When used up, a "ceremony of replacement" must be performed, and a new implement consecrated, or the old image "restored" (a "rescuing of what is worn out").[18]

Our third category, "implements for ritual," ranges from the natural stone object found to embody Vishnu (no. 16) to its lotus-stand (no. 17), bells (no. 24), water vessels (no. 21), lamps (no. 22) and other tools for priests; from man-made images of deities and saints that attend in home shrines (nos. 18–20) to water-pots that can either be the focus of ritual or perform it (nos. 30, 31); to Manasa water-pots visibly manifesting snake-deities, which have functioned in rural agrarian rituals over many centuries (no. 29). These implements—through light, incense, sound, and vision—help effect a mental state in the worshiper that is the actual "image" of worship. They also are sometimes worshiped before use. To paraphrase Davis, the object and its user never exist in an unconsecrated state.

The fourth category, "utensils," represents plates (nos. 32, 34, 36), bowls (nos. 33, 35), rice measures (no. 39), cutters (no. 40), and other implements of household activity that may be used for ritual cooking and presentation as much as for home use. Bamboo mats (nos. 43–46) form ornamented seats in the home or the home shrine, neither restricted, in Danto's terms, to being "thick with significance" nor merely objects of "sustained utility."[19]

"Architecture and ornament" includes components of larger home shrines and wooden images that can be used as decoration in the home. Yet also here we include the painted lids of large rice-storage jars that make the goddess visible, are placed as one of the foci for worship on the altar of a home shrine for certain rituals, and then may be used to ornament the house (nos. 56–58). Between container and contained is a difference not of matter but of thought.

Our final category, "votive objects and toys," intentionally crosses play and ritual, in part to emphasize that every ritual is play and all objects are votive to the thoughts they signify. Here again the context of use tells us more than the inherited forms. For every object there may be multiple textual and interpretive communities. Clients and craftsmen interact in significant sodalities, one group providing objects to be consumed by other groups to fit their own sets of understanding and utility. If "wire-wax" techniques seem in many instances tribal, for example, their practitioners represent a variety of communities and economic compromises. Categories of utility, broadly focused, define the reception and production of art. Yet objects can both embody thought and dematerialize it through varieties of reception. Art or artifact?

> As wing to bird,
> water to fish,
> life to the living—
> so you to me.
> But tell me, Mahadeva, beloved,
> who are you?
> Who are you, really?
> Vidyapati says, They are one another.[20]

As Edward Dimock points out in his essay in this catalogue, drawing on the *Taitirriya Upanishad*, "*brahman* [the cosmic spirit] is food. . . . Mankind is food for death; he is nourished and nourishes; I who am food eat the eater of food."[21]

In exploring the art of home ritual and the ritual of artistic display in this exhibition, "Cooking for the Gods," let us liberate our categories. In the terms of structuralist theory, let the raw be cooked, and the cooked raw.[22]

NOTES

1. Sunday, January 8, 1995, section 2, p. 37; *The New York Times Book Review,* ibid., p. 24; Arthur C. Danto, "Artifact and Art," in *ART/artifact: African Art in Anthropology Collections* (New York: The Center for African Art, 1988).
2. Danto, p. 29.
3. Danto, p. 31.
4. Op. cit., Sec. 2, p. 36.

5. Cited in Wayne Koestenbaum, "Obscenity: A Celebration," *The New York Times Magazine*, May 21, 1995, p. 47.

6. See, for example, Franz Boas, *Primitive Art* (Cambridge, MA: Harvard University Press, 1927), and the early twentieth-century "World of Art" series for which Ananda Coomaraswamy wrote *The Arts and Crafts of India and Ceylon* (London: T. N. Foulis, 1913).

7. Richard Davis, "Loss and Recovery of Ritual Self Among Hindu Images," *Journal of Ritual Studies* vol. 6, no. 1 (1992):48.

8. *The American Heritage Dictionary of the English Language, New College Edition* (Boston: Houghton Mifflin Company, 1979), p. 74, gives as its principal definition "Human effort to imitate, supplement, alter, or counteract the work of nature."

9. Danto, p. 29.

10. *Making Things in South Asia: The Role of Artist and Craftsman*, edited by Michael W. Meister (Philadelphia: Department of South Asia Regional Studies, 1988).

11. Stella Kramrisch, "Artist, Patron, and Public in India," *The Far Eastern Quarterly* (May 1956), reprinted in *Exploring India's Sacred Art, Selected Writings of Stella Kramrisch*, edited by Barbara Stoller Miller (Philadelphia: University of Pennsylvania Press, 1983), p. 60.

12. Michael W. Meister, "Indian Seeing and Western Knowing: An Art Historian's Perspective," in *Sri Nagabhinandanam* (Dr. M. S. Nagarajarao Festschrift) (Bangalore: Dr. M. S. Nagarajarao Felicitation Committee, 1995).

13. Danto, p. 24. His discussion is of distinctions between "pot people" and "basket folk."

14. Kathleen Ashley, "Art in Ritual Context: Introduction," *Journal of Ritual Studies* vol. 6, no. 1 (1992):1–11, citing also Mieke Bal and Norman Bryson, "Semiotics in Art History," *The Art Bulletin* 73 (1991):174–208.

15. Davis, p. 51.

16. Dinitia Smith, "Will the New Chief of the Modern Keep It Modern?," *The New York Times*, National Edition, Thursday, June 15, 1995, pp. B1, B7.

17. Davis, p. 51; for a recent discussion of the ambiguities of museum display of Asian traditional and contemporary art, see Vishakha N. Desai, "Re-Visioning Asian Arts in the 1990s: Reflections of a Museum Professional" (in "A Range of Critical Perspectives: The Problematics of Collecting and Display, part 2"), *The Art Bulletin* 77 (1995): 169–174.

18. Davis, pp. 52–53.

19. Stella Kramrisch, *Unknown India: Ritual Art in Tribe and Village* (Philadelphia: Philadelphia Museum of Art, 1968).

20. From Edward C. Dimock, "*Bhakti*," in this volume.

21. Dimock, in this volume.

22. Let us resist, as Marshall Sahlins warns, "imperialist hegemony masquerading as subaltern resistance." Cited in Richard Bernstein's review of Sahlins, *How 'Natives' Think About Captain Cook, for Example* (Chicago: Chicago University Press, 1995), in *The New York Times*, May 24, 1995. See Claude Levi-Strauss, *The Raw and the Cooked*, translated from the French by John and Doreen Wightman (New York: Harper & Row, 1969); Fine Young Cannibals, "The raw & the cooked" (Miami: CPP/Belwin, 1989).

An alter to Lakshmi uses a painted rice-pot cover to invoke the goddess of prosperity. Sheaves of un-husked rice and sugarcane stalks suggest nature's fertility.

Rice patterns are painted on the floor and a water-pot is placed at the center of the design to call forth the deity.

Household Ritual
and Women's
Domains

PIKA GHOSH

Whereas the priest presides in the temple, the women preside in the home, where they perform most religious and social rituals without the mediation of a priest. The sacred geography of the home centers in the kitchen, where food for the family and the household gods is prepared. Women keep the kitchen clean and pure to avoid that germs, dust, and other kinds of pollution spoil the food.[1] The kitchen floor and counters are thoroughly cleaned, and the ingredients that go into the meal are sorted and carefully prepared. Women who work in the kitchen ready themselves by removing footwear before entering the kitchen. They may also bathe, put on clean clothes, and tie their hair back before beginning to cook the meal. The preservation of the purity in the kitchen becomes a daily ritual and is analogous to the purity associated with a temple; the preparation of food is regarded as an act of worship similar to rituals performed by a priest.

Purity standards maintained in the kitchen make it an appropriate space for setting up the family shrine. The ritual activities performed at the altar, in turn, go toward transforming what might be seen as a profane space into a sacred one. This conflation of spaces reinforces the close association of worship with daily domestic activities.

Women assume responsibility for conveying the transfer of divine beneficence that occurs during the offering and blessing of food. The woman who cooks the food also utters a *mantra* over it and serves it to the family members as if she were the priest. At the moment of chanting the *mantra*, she also invokes the sacredness of the location and calls the deity to preside. Women make this invitation even as they become the conduit for the transference of potency. This, in turn, empowers women to conduct other rituals such as the rites at a marriage with an authority analogous to that of a priest.

In many of the ritual performances, such as the observance of vows no priest is necessary, and women assume the role of the Brahmin as intercessors to the household gods. There are other rituals conducted primarily by the women of the family whose only request is that the priest initiate the ritual by touching the central object, image, or person. After this, he is no longer needed. Lina Fruzzetti has observed this balance between women and the priest as performers of ritual, writing: "women and the Brahmin priest are ritualists in different contexts. When the one is the chief ritualist, the other is absent."[2] In rituals conducted by the priest in the household, the women often assist him, regardless of whether they are themselves from the Brahmin castes or not. They clean utensils, sweep the floor, prepare food offerings, and during the performance they hand him implements, light lamps, and so on.

The vows (*brata*) taken by girls and young brides, however, are exclusively an activity for women. These rituals rigidly exclude all men from participating or even observing them in their performance.[3] These vows are dedicated to powerful nature spirits or deities and take the form of contracts between them and the young woman. The young woman resolves to perform a sacred act to please the deity, who, in turn, grants her request.

The woman is able to approach the deity directly with her personal requests: the safety of a brother, the health of a child, a good husband, the desire for beautiful ornaments, or good weather for the rice harvest.[4] These vows allow women to voice their day-to-day concerns for their families, homes, and good health, a higher living standard or social status, perils and evils; the vows also allow women to cope with their most personal anxieties such as barrenness or widowhood, conditions threatening their position of authority within the family.

The allegiance given to the deities in these vows are not the high gods and goddesses of the Hindu pantheon, but rather the folk deities and spirits who are believed to interact with women in their everyday lives. For instance, Manasa, the goddess who showers her snakes on the damp earth during the monsoon season must be appeased in order to protect against snake bite. For the same reason, snakes are offered bowls of milk to avert their attention from human beings.[5]

Instead of worshiping deities embodied in metal or stone images as in the temple, these rituals often focus on patterns made on the earthen floor using a rice-flour paste by which the deity or spirit is invoked. Kramrisch has described particularly well the potency of these rice-paste designs (alpana):

> The sun, the moon, the stars, the earth are integrated in them and also the things desired by the young girl who draws them, ornaments, a mirror and the like; and the whole cosmos is conjured up to bless and fulfill a young girl's wish—for even a simple wish is not to be fulfilled if no effort is made at the right time to communicate with the powers that work in heaven and on earth. Here is the magic circle, in other designs the sacred square, a concatenation of curves or an intersection of polygons, that encloses the magic field. Into it the power of a god is invoked. It is assigned to its enclosure, it is spellbound. It cannot escape; it is controlled. It is held in its confinement, bound in the plane by the outline of the enclosure so that it cannot escape into the ground.[6]

During the brata dedicated to Lakshmi, the goddess of wealth and prosperity, a variety of motifs are created on the floor such as lotus blossoms, fish, paired footprints that mark the arrival of the goddess, and objects such as necklaces, conch-shell bangles, hand mirrors, and cosmetic containers filled with vermilion (sindoor). These are objects that are frequently used by married women and are thought to be auspicious. They please the goddess and gain her assistance in driving out evil, poverty, and misery from the precincts of the home.[7]

These vows are solemn acts requiring high standards of purity such as fasting, bathing, chastity, and adhering to a prescribed order of activities. The sequence of activities that are part of the vow are as follows:

> At first a desire grows in the mind, the object is then drawn, modelled and decorated, and at last it is expressed in spells. First the desire, then the spell (chhada) and in the end, the story (katha) or history—all these complete a brata.[8]

These activities differ from those of temple or festival worship where priests preside. Instead of the incantation of verses from scriptures, vows include the recitation of folk rhymes and the retelling of stories from Puranas and from women's own lives and experiences. The words for these rhymes and stories are not written but are part of an oral tradition that is handed down from mother to daughter, mother-in-law to daughter-in-law. As a result, "we see in these bratas a true picture of the woman's heart—her desires, fancies and imaginations—a great worship of life unlike the ceremonial worship alleged to be based on the scriptures."[9]

While observances of vows are understood as a separate women's activity, certain rituals led by women supplement those conducted by the priest. One situation that exemplifies the interrelationship between women's and priestly rituals is the Bengali marriage ceremony. One without the other is incomplete.

As demonstrated by the numerous correspondences between the objects, actions, words, and ideas that constitute the rituals conducted by women and priests, acts by the married kinswomen of the bride and groom must be understood as parallel to those of the priest. The turmeric smearing ritual performed by women on the morning of the wedding, for example, is complemented by the ritual smearing of vermilion sindoor powder on the bride's hair by the groom during the evening ceremony, led by the priest.

On the morning of the wedding, the turmeric ceremony initiates the sequence of activities that confers on the young bride her married status. Married women of the kin group gather around the bride and rub a paste of turmeric and oil into her skin. This mixture is provided by the women of the groom's family. Thus women of both kin groups actively participate in cleansing and purifying the bride for marriage.[10] Following this ritual, her head is covered with the end of her sari, an act associated with married women.[11] The ritual is considered an auspicious marker of the bride's change of status. She will become a wife just as the women who perform the ritual.

During the evening, the priest conducts the bride's transference from father to groom. At this time, the groom receives her by smearing vermilion powder in her hair. The priest then covers the bride's hair with a sari just as the women had covered her in the morning after the turmeric rite. The priest then performs a rite invoking Agni, the god of fire, to witness the bride's move from her father's family to that of her husband's.

Women and priests have complementary functions in the marriage ceremony. While priests invoke the high gods, women perform rituals as wives and mothers.

Kinswomen bless a bride during her turmeric smearing ritual.

They derive authority to do so from very different sources:

> The Brahman is a ritualist by virtue of his purity and position in caste hierarchy; women are ritualists in the same manner, performing the same acts, because of the meaning of marriage in Bengali life. Just as the Brahman invokes the gods in a *puja* so too do the women invoke the goddess in the bride and divinize bride and groom as a combined male/female category, expressing a basic complementarity in Bengali society. Women do this in accordance with the sacredness of marriage and the central role of the married woman in the *sangsar* of caste, kinship, and household.[12]

The household rituals that women perform derive their authority from their marital status and fertility. In Bengal, the notion of both sacredness and auspiciousness is intimately associated with women. The newly married woman is introduced to her husband's house as a deity, not just as a wife. Bengali terms for *wife* are applied to Lakshmi, the goddess of wealth and prosperity, and the Bengali woman is described as being Lakshmi because she is the embodiment of the virtues of the goddess.

Being a wife and mother is the condition for performing rituals in the home. Her status is preserved and protected by such life-affirming rituals as celebrations of menstruation, marriage, pregnancy, childbirth, and widowhood. These rituals not only mark the transitions from one stage to another, but also sanctify the woman at each; they restore the purity of the woman, and through her role as the giver of birth, that of the family and kin group as well.[13]

The transitions experienced by women from one stage in life to the next are made auspicious by rituals performed by women of the larger family group. When a girl reaches puberty, for example, she is considered ready to be married, but since most weddings are not arranged until much later, her fertility is safeguarded by the powers of the goddesses invoked during menstrual rites. The presence of an unmarried young woman in the home, however, creates a potential for incest, a dangerously impure act. Menstrual rituals

Kinswomen dress the bride and place coral and shell bracelets on her wrist.

The bride and groom are dressed in auspicious garments for the evening ceremony.

thus are also intended to reinstate a condition of purity by establishing significant parallels between menstruation and marriage. By so doing, the auspiciousness of the married state can be extended symbolically to the former impure state.[14]

One menstrual rite requires the girl to sit on the floor, holding either a set of grinding stones or a mortar and pestle on her lap, while prayers of blessing are chanted by older women in the family. The same utensils are also held by the bride during the marriage ceremony and later used in the kitchen to grind spices. This ritual reflects directly on the role of the young girl as a future bride and wife. The explicitly sexual symbolism of the grinding stones and the mortar and pestle also anticipates her wifely duty of bearing children who will continue the family line.[15]

These utensils are associated with Shasthi, the goddess who presides over childbirth and protects newborn children. Women worship her in the form of paired grinding stones after the birth of any child. Menstrual rites can be seen, then, as a means to restore purity to a girl by celebrating her potential for attaining marriage and motherhood.

Another rite of passage concerns a woman's journey into widowhood, an irreversible and inauspicious condition. The shift from wife to widow on the death of a husband is accomplished through a ritual in which the symbols of the wedding are evoked. The bathing of a new widow parallels the marriage bath after the application of turmeric.[16] As with the bride, a new widow is assisted by the women of her father's family in this bathing ritual. A first set of widow's clothing is provided by her father's family just as they had provided clothing at the time of her marriage. Along with the *sari*, the widow is presented a garland of fragrant white flowers, just as the bride was garlanded. These associations between the rituals of widowhood and marriage help protect the woman at a vulnerable time of life.

Through these elaborate religious and social rituals, as well as the more modest daily ones of cutting vegetables, grinding spices, cooking, fetching water, picking flowers, worshiping the gods, singing folk songs, stitching quilts, and weaving mats, women create their own identity. Their authority to perform such household rituals derives from the significant roles they play in Bengali society as wives and mothers.

NOTES

1. For a detailed discussion of purity and pollution regulations, see Lawrence Babb, *The Divine Hierarchy* (New York, Columbia University Press, 1975), p. 105.

2. Lina Fruzzetti, *The Gift of a Virgin: Women, Marriage, and Ritual in a Bengali Society* (New Brunswick, NJ: Rutgers University Press, 1982), p. 69.

3. See Tapanmohan Chatterji, *Alpana* (Bombay: Orient Longmans, 1948), p. 1.

4. Abanindranath Tagore, *Banglar Brata* (Calcutta: Visvabharati, 1947).

5. Ibid.

6. Stella Kramrisch, *Unknown India: Ritual Art in Tribe and Village* (Philadelphia: Philadelphia Museum of Art, 1968), pp. 65–66.

7. Chatterji, pp. 34–35.

8. Chatterji, pp. 34–35.

9. Chatterji, p. 4.

10. Through this ritual, women purify the young bride. The use of turmeric paste for cleansing of her skin is similar to the use of other cleansing agents such as witch hazel.

11. For a discussion of the ritual significance of covering the head with the *sari* and *purdah*, see Mary Higdon Beech, "The Domestic Realm in the Lives of Hindu Women in Calcutta," in *Separate Worlds: Studies of Purdah in South Asia*, edited by Hanna Papanek and Gail Minault (Delhi: Chanakya Publications, 1982), p. 116.

12. Fruzzetti, p. 69.

13. Lineage is conceptualized in Bengali terms as having issued from the father's line. It is therefore of great importance to the lineage that the fertility and sanctity of the woman be protected.
See Fruzzetti, pp. 120–121. She has noted one metaphor that parallels a marriage to planting seed in the field.
See also Beech, pp. 113–114.

14. Fruzzetti, p. 96. She has noted that these menstrual rites are even known as *anna biye* ("another marriage") and *natun biye* ("new marriage"), suggesting the deliberate connection being made between menstruation and the later secure status of marriage.

15. Such menstrual rites have been described by Fruzzetti, pp. 96–99.

16. For a discussion of these ritual activities, see Fruzzetti, pp. 105–107.

The Keshta Raya temple in Bishnupur (A.D. 1655) *mimics vernacular village hut forms.*

Bhakti

EDWARD C. DIMOCK

The word *bhakti*, which is usually translated as "devotion," is derived from the Sanksrit stem /bhaj-, which means "share in, participate in"; the sharing is of experience, or of food, and in one of the epic texts the word is used to mean specifically, "meal."

The connection between the sharing of food and religious ritual experience is not uncommon; there are qualities of intimacy and personal immediacy between them. It is true that the theology, psychology, and philosophy of the *bhakti* of the Bengali Vaishnavas (the name is derived from the classical god Vishnu, despite the fact that Krishna, who in some other traditions is only one of many manifestations of Vishnu, is here the high god) are characterized by abstruse and complex theory. But there are other aspects of the system that are domestic or, at the temple, expressed in congregational worship in the passionate and often very beautiful songs called *kirtana* ("praise"). These hymns celebrate the many facets of the life of Krishna, and especially his love affairs with Radha and the other *gopis*, of which more will be said.

Many scholars have been drawn in to the complexities of the theology, and the domestic aspects of *bhakti* have been too often overlooked, but it is significant that in many households there are daily family-bounded activities having to do primarily with the kitchen and, not surprisingly, with the gods' room, where the family deities stay, honored members of the household who participate as a matter of course in its life.

The kitchen is of primary importance because here, as in many cultures, the religious significance of food—the rituals of the sharing of it and the meaning of this, the proper methods of its preparation and consumption—is of very great import. In some other cultures the simplest and most common of domestic rituals is the blessing of the food before its consumption—the

saying of grace. In Bengal, as in other parts of Hindu India, this concern is very much more elaborate.

There is a social dimension in the communal meals that are a part of this as of many cultures. In the Christian tradition, this ranges from the *agapae* of early Christianity, those communal feasts held before the Lord's Supper, at which Christians of all ranks would, as a gesture of love and solidarity, break bread together, to the church suppers of contemporary small-town America. Among the Vaishnavas of Bengal, in the sixteenth century and today, communal supping is of very great ritual and social importance. For among the very important ritual acts that a *bhakta*, a follower of the way of *bhakti*, must carry out are the association of other devoted Vaishnavas and partaking of food offered to God, as we shall see. The major doctrinal text of the tradition, the *Caitanya-caritamrta*, a very long theological biography, written by one Krishnadasa Kaviraja probably in 1615 A.D., in the course of interpreting the life of the great revivalist and religious leader Caitanya (1486–1533 A.D.), is filled with passages describing religious occasions, and feasts are inevitable parts of them. These passages are often very long, sometimes hundreds of lines, and the food is described in great and loving detail. But even when no particular occasion presents itself, the preparation of food for offering to God or to a revered one, a *guru*, is a matter of significance. In the following excerpt, a female follower of Caitanya, by the name of Damayanti, who lived in Caitanya's home town of Navadvipa, in Bengal, prepares food to send to him in Puri, in Orissa, where he has taken up residence in that great Vaishnava center (*CC, antya-lila* 10:12–34):

. . . . Damayanti had prepared many things, wonderful things to eat, proper food for Prabhu [i.e., "the Lord," Caitanya], so many that he could eat for a

Top: Vishnu, invoked in a shalagrama *stone placed on a bell-metal stand, is joined by his consort Lakshmi, invoked in a pot filled with water.*

Above: Pots lined with leaves, fruit, and flowers, are filled with water, and painted with vermilion sindoor *paste. They are worshiped as the goddess.*

year; there were preparations of green mangoes and ginger and hot chutneys, and all kinds of dried fruits and fruits fried in oil [?], and *amata* [?] and jute leaves powdered with great care. . . . Prabhu understood the affection [with which it had been prepared], being sensitive to the inner emotion, and took great delight in the chutneys and powdered leaves. Damayanti considered Prabhu as human [and reasoned]: Sometimes phlegm forms in the belly because of heavy food; if then one eats jute leaves, that phlegm is destroyed. . . . She powdered coriander and anise and mixed them with husked rice and made them into balls and coated them with sugar. And separately she spiced balls of rice with dried ginger, and put them into sacks made of cloth, with jujube prepared in various ways, and coconuts and butter and sweet things and preparations of powdered camphor and black pepper and cardamom and cloves and roasted sugar and. . . .[1]

When the food did not have to be shipped long distances, of course, and could be served immediately, it could be proportionately more elaborate. The most important aspect of the passage, however, is that the food was prepared with love. Care and thoughtfulness in the preparation of food is, even in the nonreligious context, a mark of affection. Caitanya, who was considered to be not only *guru* but the manifest Krishna, understood completely.

There are many ways in which the personal relates to the cosmic. In some systems of thought, the body is the microcosm, and sustenance for it both physical and spiritual is also sustenance for the universe. The person, the home, the society are all reflections of a cosmic integration and order. The mighty god Agni is also the hearth-fire, the insurer of the continuity of family and community; Agni is also the sacrificial fire that carries offerings of butter to the realm of the gods and the cremation fire, linking mankind to the gods and to the ancestors; the fire too binds mankind in to the rest of the phenomenal world, to the sun whose light

and warmth are the sources of life itself, and to the lightning. The hearth-fire is thus at once a powerful symbol and an actual manifestation of certain truths of human life. The place where it is kept is thus to be revered and to be physically and ritually clean and pure at all times; no impure foods, or impure people, or utensils (only certain kinds of metal can be used) can be allowed in the kitchen. The food prepared there not only sustains life, but at the same time constitutes a danger, for with food the external world is taken within. The external world is a place fraught with potential disaster, and care must be taken lest its impurity be absorbed and internalized. So contagious is this danger that it can be conveyed by a glance; for as we shall see again, in some Indian thought a look is the equivalent of a touch, and has the same power to pollute or purify.

Sustenance for the body, then, is nothing less than sustenance of the universe. The idea called *dharma* is that the actions of any individual affect all the structures of which the individual is a part: one does one's duty as that duty is defined in the lawbooks (*dharmashastra*), the social structure functions smoothly, and that is reflected in the continuity of the cosmos. Some pre-Hindu texts are explicit about the matter as it related to food. The third chapter of the text called *Taitirriya Upanishad* (one of the earlier *upanishads*, usually assigned to the period between 700 and 600 B.C.), in the course of a discussion of the learning of the five phases of *brahman*, the essential spiritual principle, puts the matter thus:

Having performed austerity, he understood that Brahma[n] is food. For truly, indeed, beings here are born from food, when born they live by food, on deceasing they enter into food; mankind is food for death; he is nourished and nourishes; I, who am food, eat the eater of food! I have overcome the whole world.[2]

The *bhakta* sees many such types of relationships between the personal and the cosmic; they appear also in the realms of the esthetic and the theological, and it is here that in the minds of many the term *bhakti* is virtually synonymous with that branch of modern Hinduism called Vaishnava.

The primary deity of the Vaishnavas in Bengal is the charming, beautiful cowherd lad Krishna (considered in some other parts of India as only one of several manifestations of the high god of Vishnu, in Bengal he himself is the high god). The stories about Krishna, on which a whole complex theology is constructed, are ones of idyllic beauty, pastoral serenity, and simple, unaffected, and very human love.

These stories are told in many places, but perhaps the most important one is the Tenth Book of the *Bhagavata Purana*, a Sanskrit text of perhaps the tenth century A.D., thought to originate in South India. The stories told in the text are of village life, of the unrestrained play and affection of the youth Krishna and his friends as they tended the cattle in the place called Vrindavana on the banks of the beautiful river Yamuna; they are stories of the love that Krishna's foster parents bore for him; and the most important stories are those of the unqualified and unselfish, and highly erotic, love felt for Krishna by the cowherd girls, the *gopis*, of the village (it was not until later that these *gopis* were epitomized by one named Radha, who still later became the symbol of the human soul longing for God).

Interpretation of this scripture (it is scripture in the sense that it is revelation of that which takes place eternally in a heavenly Vrindavana) is that it presents an allegory of the proper attitudes of mankind toward God. These four in number (or five, if you count, as some theologians do, that attitude called *shanta*, "peace," which comes when the *bhakta* recognizes the deity as eternal and infinitely grand, while he the *bhakta* is an insignificant and minute observer of the grandeur). They are called *dasya*, which is the feeling that a servant has toward a master—repectful, somewhat distant but still of decided intimacy; *sakhya*, the emotions that friends feel toward friends—teasing, familiar, sometimes even rough, as were Krishna's young cowherd friends as they laughed and wrestled and played with him and with each other on the river's bank; *vatsalya*, love between parents and children, that love that Krishna's foster parents held toward him—protective, proud, sometimes irritated and sometimes awed—and he toward them; and the best of all, *madhurya*, "sweetness," the erotic, passionate, yearning, sometimes jealous love that the *gopis*, and later especially Radha, felt for him. *Shanta* aside, these sets of feelings share an extreme intimacy; together they constitute an ascending series, each including the characteristics of the one before it. Thus *madhurya* encompasses humility, playfulness, and protectiveness and adds its own erotic quality. It is thus the most intimate, the most complex and intense, and thus the most satisfying form of love to both the *bhakta* and Krishna. The love between lover and beloved on the human plane, then, is thus the paradigm of the highest kind of relationship that a human being can have with God. That there is throughout an element of sacrifice should also be noted, for true love is such only if it can be given without thought of the satisfaction of the self. Only when the heart is given unconditionally to a lover or to God is such love pure and thus efficacious.

This attitude of the *bhakta* as lover of Krishna is the one most often depicted in painting and in dance and drama. The stories of the *gopis* are intense, immediate, psychologically complex, and thus natural subjects, especially, of the dance. The dance form called Odissi, for instance, is a dramatic form with elaborate sets of gestures of hands, bodies, feet, and eyes representing the intricacies of the love affair in all its emotions and subtleties. So complex are these representations that proper interpretation and thus appreciation of them depend as much on the knowledge and sophistication of the audience as of the performer.

The Bengali Vaishnava system of thought, uniquely, pays a great deal of attention to the arts and to esthetic experience, for they consider it to be identical with the religious one. They are both conditions in which one is abstracted from this world and established in another one. As with the English Metaphysical poets and with the Ignatian Exercises, one creates and experiences poetry, for instance, only when one is in a proper religious condition. The true *bhakta*, the lover of God, is also the true poet.

It is thus perhaps not surprising that poetry and song are justifiably considered to be the most outstanding expressions of the religious tradition. The poet serves both as observer of the love, and actual love-making, of the *gopis* and Krishna, and thus describer of it, but also, as a *bhakta*, he is a participant in it. The following poem, a song, really, by a poet who lived possibly before Caitanya, is a good example of it, and shows the poet's dual role:

As the mirror to my hand,
flowers to my hair,
kohl to my eyes,
tambul to my mouth,
musk to my breast,
necklace to my throat,
ecstacy to my flesh,
heart to my home—

as wing to bird,
water to fish,
life to the living—
so you to me.
But tell me,
Madhava, beloved,
who are you?

Who are you, really?

Vidyapati says, They are one another.[3]

While this *madhurya* mode is the best and most satisfying to the *bhakta* and to Krishna, it is perhaps most appropriate for devotees of an ecstatic bent. For most people, for daily and domestic religious expression, perhaps the *vatsalya* attitude is better—the attitude which puts the *bhakta* in a parental relationship to Krishna. Stemming from it are such activities as feeding and dressing the deity, putting him to rest in the evening and awakening him in the morning, and so on. Food is prepared and offered at appropriate times, and these offerings are very important daily activities, and are called *prasada*. The term, in addition to referring to the offering itself, has a meaning very close to "blessing" or even "grace." For the food offered to and accepted by the deity is touched by him, and thus when it is distributed to and eaten by the *bhaktas* it has assumed a sacred quality. It is in fact the *ucchishta*, the "leftovers" of the deity's meal. This too has interesting and complex implications, for it is a way of stating relationships between the human, or social, and the divine planes. In ordinary social intercourse the leftovers of someone else's meal are impure. The notion behind *prasada* is of course that such social prohibitions do not apply when the context is religious, or more extremely, that social prohibitions must be breached when the context is religious. It is parallel to the poetic and religious statement that says that some of the *gopis*, and Radha herself, are betrothed or married to others at the time when they carry on their affair with Krishna, a condition that certainly would not be condoned in a normal social situation. The eating of the leftovers of someone else's plate is also an expression of great humility, as is the placing of the dust from someone's feet on one's head, and it

is usually only a deity or a *guru* who is so honored. The act is one of great devotion, and one of sacrifice, a definition of the social order in which the self is placed last.

This definition is even more striking than is obvious in the consumption of leftover food. For *prasada* is actually the same substance of which the deity has partaken: it has not only been accepted in some mysterious way, but has actually been partially eaten. That the amount of food offered has not been physically diminished after the deity has partaken is not significant, for just as the deity is made up of nonmaterial qualities, so he has feasted on that part of the offering which is nonmaterial, leaving the rest to be consumed by material people. Perhaps that is the love with which the food was prepared, and which Caitanya, "sensitive to the inner emotion," understood. Food, like everything else, consists of *gunas*, the qualities which give an object its distinctness. Physical *gunas* give rise to form, distinguishing one object from another. And coterminous with these *gunas* is a set of nonphysical ones, which lend an object its essence. It is essence, not form, that is intrinsic, nourishing, and pleasing to God. It nourishes the soul, too, which is what people share with God. Unfortunately, there is also an animal side to our nature, and that requires substantial and not spiritual sustenance.

Bhakti is not the exclusive preserve of the Vaishnavas, though the Vaishnava interpretation of it perhaps provides the paradigm. But the social manifestations of the Vaishnava theology, which include a kind of puritanism, austerity, intellectualism, and, of course, strict vegetarianism, do not completely define the Bengali religious scene. Many people in Bengal consider the goddess, in one or another of her many forms and names, to be the high deity. The great festivals of Bengal are her festivals, and Bengalis of all persuasions

participate in them. The great autumnal festival of the goddess Durga, for instance, is a time for both domestic and public observance, and families of all religious traditions gather and exchange gifts and feast together and wear new clothes. But at these festivals one of the major differences between the Vaishnavas and the Shaktas, as the worshipers of the goddess are called, becomes clear. For the goddess is pleased by blood, and goats are sacrificed to her by her devotees. After identical types of ritual preparation for the sacrifice, the Vaishnavas will decapitate a gourd.

The term *Shakta* is from the Sanskrit *shakti*, which means "power," and indeed the goddess is energy: one famous icon represents her dancing upon the inert prostrate form of her consort Shiva. In this icon she is usually Kali (the name means both "black," which is indeed her color, and "time" or "death"), her long red tongue hanging out of her mouth, a sword in one hand and the severed head of a demon in another, a garland of heads around her neck and another around her waist: she is altogether so fearsome that there is a reluctance on the part of some to categorize her worship together with that of the Vaishnavas, as *bhakti*. But although the *bhakti* of the goddess is perhaps more earthy and less idealized, less intellectual, perhaps less complex, and certainly less gentle, there is the same immediacy and very real intimacy about it. The element of love, caring, and nourishment, is very much, though in a different way, present.

While the Vaishnavas posit four (or five) types of relationships between the *bhakta* and God, the Shaktas have, for all intents and purposes, three. The first is that of a child toward its mother, and the best known of the Shakta songs speak with the voice of that child, wheedling, cajoling, scolding, blaming, and thanking its mother for protection, nourishment, and love, or for the lack of these. One of the most famous of the Shakta poets was Ramprasad Sen (b. 1718), and this song is typical of him and of the genre:

> I'll no longer call you Mother,
> for all the pain you've given me,
> and still give me.
> Once I had a home.
> Now you've made me a beggar.
> What else do you have in store for me?
> You have me begging for my food
> from door to door.
> When the Mother leaves,
> how does the child live?
> Ramprasad was the child of his Mother,
> but you, O Mother, are your child's
>   enemy.
> When his Mother's near,
> and still her child suffers so,
> tell me, what good is such a Mother?[4]

Ramprasad has, somewhat like the *gopis*, given up the security of the householder life for religious love and, like a child, is angry and disappointed because his reward is not immediate. Such songs are, it must also be remembered, in a total context of great psychological complexity, and other songs speak of the warmth the child feels in the warmth of the Mother's love.

A second type of song, also in the *vatsalya* mode, is that in which the *bhakta* is the parent and the goddess is the child called Uma. These songs are called *agamani* songs, "welcome" songs, and they are sung at that part of the Durga *puja* when the goddess is the daughter of every Bengali household returning from her husband's house for her annual visit to her parents. The songs greet Uma as a young bride returning from the house of her husband Shiva, high in the Himalayas:

> O Uma, you have finally, kindly
> come from the place of snows!
> Come, give me a hug!
> At the end of the rains we lost you,
> our hearts were like stones
> with grief, the house
> was empty.
> But we no longer suffer,
> now we live again,
> saying your name, O Durga,

> over and again!
> Come, my daughter, let me hold you to
>   my heart,
> and extinguish the grief
> I felt at my child's loss.
> Let me look at your face,
> the full moon,
> young bride of Shiva,
> let me call you "daughter."
> The fire of my sorrow was very hot
> but now it is extinguished.[5]

The songs of her departure, after her brief visit, are proportionately sad.

There is a third mode of relating to the goddess, and like the *shanta* mode of the Vaishnavas, there is some question as to whether or not it should be included with the gentler, more intimate forms of *bhakti*. This is the view of the goddess as fierce and ferocious, albeit protective, and to be propitiated. This is the goddess who requires blood sacrifice, and awe, rather than love, on the part of the *bhakta*. This goddess is Death. But, the Shaktas ask, since Death is the Mother, how can there be fear?

> What more fear do I have of Death?
> For Kali, the Destroyer of Death,
> has wakened in my heart!
> At whose feet the Lord of Death
> himself has fallen,
> what can paltry death do,
> when that Kali's near,
> at the end of time?
> Panchanan offers himself
> at the feet of the Dark One.
> He knows that the God of Death
> is as a straw, and he
> has conquered death.[6]

The sacrifice, called *balidan*, is usually of black male goats, perfectly formed, with perfect markings. The animal is dedicated to the goddess and, while it is in a peaceful state because of that dedication, is decapitated. The meat is distributed among the worshipers, cooked, and eaten as *prasada* (it might be noted that some people who are otherwise vegetarian feel that animal flesh taken under these religious circumstances is not impure). Such animal

sacrifices are not inexpensive, and are performed domestically usually only at the great celebrations of the goddess (Durga *Puja* or Kali *Puja*), but take place many times a day at her temples; there is great merit attached to offering an animal in *balidan*, and people will bring animals to the temple in fulfillment of vows or to seek some special or general blessing from the goddess.

There is great merit in it partially because the sacrifice is not only of the animal, but also of the animal part of the self. Communion, then, of the *bhakta* with the deity and with other *bhaktas*, is on the level of the pure. And we might close where we began. For although Hindu thought has never been as much given to theological dispute over such matters, and has never felt it necessary to debate questions such as those of consubstantiation vs. transubstantiation in relating to the divine through food, the meaning of sharing between the *bhakta* and the deity is very powerful indeed, and the sharing of food central, in a symbolic and in a ritual sense. The shared communal table has all the virtues of simple celebration of good fortune and enjoyment. There is always present, however, the element of sacrifice, and the awareness that love is absorbed with food, that its sustenance is on several levels, and an area in which human and divine can share.

NOTES

1. *The Caitanya-caritamrta* of Krsna-dasa Kaviraja; translated by Edward C. Dimock, edited by Tony K. Stewart; to appear as Vol. 52 of The Harvard Oriental Series.
2. R. H. Hume, translation, *The Thirteen Principal Upanishads* (Oxford University Press, 1921).
3. From Edward C. Dimock and Denise Levertov, *In Praise of Krishna*, Songs from the Bengali (Chicago: University of Chicago Press, 1981).
4. Given in slightly different form in D. C. Sen, *History of Bengali Language and Literature* (University of Calcutta Press, 1954), p. 603.
5. *Sakta padavali*, edited by Amarendranath Ray (Calcutta: University of Calcutta Press, 1955), song no 58.
6. Ibid., song no. 287.

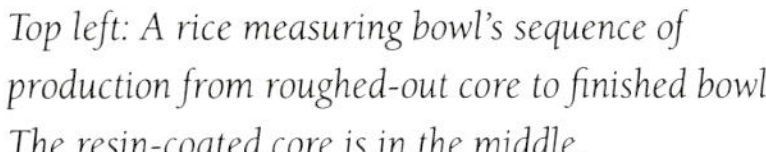

Top left: A rice measuring bowl's sequence of production from roughed-out core to finished bowl. The resin-coated core is in the middle.

Top right: Sal tree resin (dhuno) is melted and sieved to remove impurities. It will be stretched into tapes or rolled into threads, then applied to the surface of the core to make the model.

Above: A measuring-bowl core is calibrated with a measured palm-leaf strip.

Above right: Scraping a measuring-bowl core to standardize it in size and shape.

Right: Resin is wrapped around the measuring-bowl core. When the design is complete, the waxed core will be covered with layers of clay to make the mold. When the resin burns away, it leaves a space within the mold that will be filled with molten metal.

Making Metal in West Bengal

LEE HORNE

This exhibition tells the story of ritual activity and everyday life through the household objects, many of them metal, that provide for and accompany the "cooking for the gods." Yet these metal vessels, implements, and images tell not only of Bengali devotion in daily life and ritual, but of the artisan and his art. They come to the hearth or shrine with stories of their own. These stories begin when the artisan first reaches for the handful of mud that will become the core of Lakshmi's owl, the flat sheet of copper that will be bent into a graceful bowl; they take us into the lives and craft of the metal workers.[1]

Who Are the Metal Workers?

Metalworking in India is an ancient tradition. It has had more than four thousand years in which to develop the diverse complex of specialized skills we see today. Perhaps as a result of this long history, there is, even in a small region like Bengal, a confusing array of caste, subcaste, and occupational names and surnames used by or applied to metal workers. Descriptive caste or group names are not necessarily accurate indicators of occupation—casters in Nabadwip, for example, who today work only in brass, still carry the name *Kansabanik,* meaning trader in bell metal. One reason may be that in spite of the generalization that metalworking, like other crafts, is an hereditary caste activity, there is actually a great deal of occupational mobility. With changing personal, economic, and political conditions artisans may be forced to give up the trade altogether. Groups transfer their working skills from one medium to another. Even though the skills required prevent easy entry into the craft, outsiders do join in as apprentices. The "origin myths" with which metalworking groups explain how and where they learned their craft suggest a long-standing

geographical mobility as well. They often include tales of migration and dispersal that are likely to be based in historical fact.

Nevertheless, many metalworking centers and many metalworking groups have indisputably long histories. Although these artisan groups generally make a number of products, they or their workplaces become renowned for particular items: plates, for example, or a fine cup, or a special kind of pitcher or image. Artisans also specialize and may become known for their technique, as has happened to the wax-thread casters of rural and tribal areas in eastern India. Differences in product and technique have a social dimension too, enforcing group identity and marriage rules.

Whether in a great city like Calcutta, a provincial town like Bishnupur, or in smaller towns or villages scattered throughout the state, metal workers usually have their own quarters. Some, like the brasscasters in Bankura or Burdwan, have been organized into craft cooperatives. A shrinking number are still itinerant, camping in temporary sites until the local demand has been filled, and then moving on. In the city and town, items that are modestly priced or in constant demand are likely to be sold in shops in the market. (Some metal workers, or members of their metalworking group, are merchants as well as artisans.) Expensive or unusual items are specially commissioned, as they have always been, in which case the patron may supply the metal in order to guarantee its quality. In rural areas artisans may travel great distances to sell at seasonal *melas,* or fairs; they also hawk their wares in village streets, accepting broken pots or rice in exchange. And, at the opposite end of the scale, a few artisans or groups have found a tourist and international market through government and commercial middlemen and agencies.

At the end of the nineteenth century, T. N. Mukharji could still claim that copper, brass, and bronze manufacture in Bengal was a thriving industry, one not threatened by foreign competition or machine-made counterparts and fed by a flourishing agricultural economy.[2] As it turned out, this bright outlook would not last long. The twentieth century has brought hardship to handicrafts throughout India. In today's economy, few can afford the full array of metalware that was once common even in rural households. Plastic, aluminum, china, and enameled wares replace brass and bell metal in the kitchen and at the table. A prime reason is the high cost of copper alloys. Legal sources for quality metals are expensive and difficult to access. The black market is even more expensive (and illegal), and scrap metal is of increasingly poor quality.

The Story of the Malhar

The effects on metal workers of these and other changes in the surrounding economy are vividly exemplified by the Malhar of the Dariapur Artisans Cooperative, a small settlement of lost wax casters in West Bengal's Burdwan district.[3]

These artisans call themselves Malhar. They and their relatives now live in small, dispersed groups in Bihar, Orissa, and West Bengal. Their original homeland is likely to have been Chota Nagpur in Bihar; they say they have spread into their present locations over the past several hundred years. Although they speak Bengali, their mother tongue, like their group, is called Malhar, a dialect apparently resembling that spoken in the Chota Nagpur area. Before they were "discovered" and settled in a government cooperative, they led an itinerant life, traveling from village to village in small groups, camping briefly to cast, and then moving on again. Especially in demand were rice measuring bowls, containers, and "*lokkhi saj*," sets of small

images used in the worship of Lakshmi. The artisans were frequently regarded with suspicion by the settled populations, with whom they had little in common. (Although there are exceptions, metal workers on the whole have not held high positions in the Indian social system nor had easy lives.) They had and still have their own system of social order and justice. Their production cycle and local market tend to be seasonal, tied to the monsoon and to religious fairs and festivals. In gatherings, held once or twice a year, bring scattered travelers back into the fold; at these times weddings are arranged and carried out, disputes settled, and community ties renewed.

By the 1950s, conditions had deteriorated so that many of these casters were living in the direst poverty. The rising cost of brass and the shrinking market for their products had taken its toll. The deforestation in the region had cut off their access to supplementary activities such as hunting and birdcatching. The materials necessary for casting—clays, resin, beeswax, fuel—once readily available from the forest had now to be purchased.

At the time of their distress, efforts were already underway across India to rescue, support, and promote her ailing crafts. Through the efforts of craft developers and government programs, the Dariapur Malhar were organized into an artisans cooperative and settled into government-provided housing. Under the terms of the cooperative, they produce traditional items as well as adaptations commissioned for a more commercial market. A few of them have been designated Master Craftsmen by the Indian government and have participated in the Festival of India and its successors around the world. Most of them remain anonymous.

Without intervention these artisans would have been forced to give up their craft altogether. Even with intervention,

few of them are making a go of it. Most of their relatives outside the cooperative have stopped casting altogether to become itinerant tinkers.

Because they have captured the imagination of craft developers, the public, and researchers alike, the work and working conditions of these modern casters have been better studied than those of their fellow artisans who work in urban settings and in the classical traditions. On the one hand their example, while dramatic, is not typical, for they have always found themselves outside the "system." On the other hand, they illustrate well the kinds of changes that crafts face in the late twentieth century.[4] The loss of a traditional, local market has stilled the furnace and stayed the hammer of many traditional metal workers. Yet others, who provide essential ritual items or have managed to adapt to a nontraditional market, appear to thrive. Craft developers who understand the habits and organization of metalworking groups can promote what works best for them while educating and facilitating a broader market. Consumers who have learned to appreciate the qualities and history of a hand-wrought artifact are less likely to seek a commercial substitute.

Michael W. Meister reminds us that "India's strengths have lain always in her ability to adjust as well as to continue."[5]

Making Metal

The metal sculptures, vessels, and utensils in "Cooking for the Gods" are nearly all made of copper or of copper alloys—bronze, bell metal, and brass in particular. Although the term *bronze* is sometimes used to mean any copper alloy, it properly refers to a mixture of copper and tin; a 10 percent tin content is common. High tin bronze, with a tin content of 20 to 25 percent, is called bell metal because of

its sonorous quality. Brass, often confused with bronze, is an alloy of copper with 10 to 30 percent zinc. India is rich in both copper and zinc and has a venerable history in their use. Copper-based metal-working traditions begin as early as the pre-Harrapan period in the third millennium B.C.[6] While bronze is admired, however, brass has long been the more popular alloy. India was a pioneer producer of zinc; brass was in use in South Asia (at Taxila) from the fourth century B.C.; brass images were common in the Gupta period 1500 years ago.[7] Bronze alloys in contrast have always depended on distant sources of tin, and are not "native" in the sense that brass is.

German silver, a relatively recent alloy of copper, nickel, and sometimes zinc, is frequently added to metals for casting. Aluminum is also a recently available metal, common in the earth's surface but recoverable only since the late nineteenth century. Alloyed with other metals, it is eminently castable and workable. Even though it has no place in the traditional list of metals, its use is growing; many of the poorer groups of casters in the hinterland can maintain their livelihood only by casting in this most available and inexpensive metal.

Judging by the absence of broken and discarded metal objects in archaeological contexts, metal has always been treated differently from other materials. Because of its intrinsic value, it tends to be reused rather than thrown away. Because of this, the alloys in actual use today, especially those used for casting, are often mixtures of many metals. Nevertheless, the working properties of a metal are as important or more so to the artisan than its availability. Scrap metal, carefully examined for iron and other inappropriate inclusions, may be satisfactory for casting, but wrought work requires a more carefully controlled composition. Copper is easy to hammer, but hard to cast by traditional methods. Adding tin, zinc, and other metals lowers its melting temperature and makes a tougher or more malleable material. Aluminum protects against corrosion.

So it is that metals, like other materials, have physical and working properties that make them more or less attractive to the artisan working with them and the patron using the product. But materials in Indian cultures, as perhaps in all cultures, can be invested with values quite apart from their functional qualities. The color of a metal is part of its esthetic appeal, and alloys differ in color as well as in working properties. Pure copper is reddish in color. Aluminum whitens the alloy, as does tin. Low tin bronze is brownish, bell metal lighter and brighter. Brass is golden.

The five-metal alloy—copper, silver, gold, brass and lead—prescribed by the classical texts no doubt has less to do with the working properties of the mix than with the auspicious quality of the metals. In any case, for ordinary castings, such a mix is prohibitively expensive. When a patron requests it, a pellet of the precious metals may be inserted within the image; it is not truly alloyed with the rest of the metal (see the section below on casting a solid image). Among Hindus copper is specified for ritual objects and implements; it is not used for cooking and eating ware.[8] Brass and bell metal are appropriate for both ritual and everyday use. Aluminum vessels are appropriate in the kitchen, but not at the shrine. These ideas about metal guide the artisan's practice and the customer's selection.

Materials

While Bengal's own alluvial geology lacks copper or other metal ores, some of India's important copper sources lie as close as the Chota Nagpur plateau in Bihar. With its history of river commerce, Bengal has historically been well placed to receive metal from these richer sources to the west. In any case, metal workers in India today only work the metal, they do not mine or smelt it. They may or may not alloy it, depending on how much control they require over its composition. While the cast metal worker is often today forced for reasons of availability and economy to use whatever non-ferrous metal they can come by, the wrought metal worker must be more selective; as noted above, metal is less forgiving of hammering than it is of casting. There is thus more variation in the composition of cast pieces than there is in wrought or hammered ones.

A metal worker must be as knowledgeable and skilled in the other materials with which he works as he is with metal; each is critical to the success of the finished piece. Other materials needed in quantity by the caster are clays and their tempers (such as sand, rice husk, or jute) and fuel (coal, coke, or dung). Each of these plays an essential part in the success of the cast.

The nature of the tools, furnaces, and other kinds of installation depend in part on the permanence of the worksite. Itinerant casters travel with what they can carry on their backs and build their furnaces on the spot with the materials at hand. Established artisans invest in permanent, sometimes elaborate, furnaces and a range of specialized tools. Both modes will be described in the technical examples that follow.

Techniques and Knowledge

Metal can be worked in more ways than might be imagined. In its solid state, it can be beaten, stretched, and bent to shape with appropriate kinds of hammers and anvils; molten, it can be poured into molds of varying complexity. Both methods may be used in the same piece, for example one that is first cast and then incised or chased to add the decoration. After shaping, it can be polished, chiseled, chased, engraved, or inlaid. These finishing techniques are often used in combination to achieve the desired effect.

A well-finished piece does not easily reveal how it was made. An ancient and use-polished image may obliterate details of its creation and replace them with a story of its own. But if you look closely at an unworn piece, you may see striations from turning and polishing, traces of resin that mark the attachment to a polishing lathe, seams from joining, or flaws resulting from breaks in the mold.

Some concrete examples will show something of the range of techniques with which metal objects are made. All of them have counterparts in the exhibit or catalog illustrations. Included are a sheet-metal *kosha*,[9] a wrought-metal cup,[10] a water jar cast in two pieces and joined together,[11] a solid cast image,[12] and a rice measuring bowl.[13] These were chosen because they illustrate distinctive processes and products. One striking difference is that the *kosha* and bell-metal cup are actually conceived and created in the hard realities of copper and brass, while the water jar, solid cast image, and lost wax bowl are conceived and created in a non-metallic material, most often clay or wax.

The present tense is used to describe these workshops and their techniques. It must be noted that (except for the rice measuring bowl) these processes were observed in the early 1960s. And, because it is difficult to explain in words what is so easily observed, the descriptions are greatly simplified.

A **Water Vessel** (*Kosha*) (Cf. no. 21) In Bamandas Mukherjee Road, north Calcutta, is a workshop specializing in copper work. Several types of ritual vessels are produced here, and three types of ritual water vessel or *kosha*: a plain sort, with or without a turned-in edge, one with a more complicated profile that requires a great deal of skill to make, and one with a rounded bottom and less developed spout. A ladle (*kushi*) completes the *kosha-kushi* pair.

To make the *kosha*, copper sheets, cut to shape according to a pattern, are cold-hammered together on an anvil. A depression on the anvil's face curves the sheet into an approximation of the *kosha*'s general form. As the work proceeds, it must be repeatedly heated and plunged into water (annealed) so that hammering, stretching, and flattening can continue without the copper becoming brittle.

The artisan then changes over to a double-headed hammer to fold over the lip's sharp edge so that it can be held comfortably in the hand. The sharp end of the hammer is used to incise the contour lines. The base is flattened so that it may be set down as well as held. Then the *kosha* is hammered both inside and out against an angled, flat-ended stake to create the well at the bottom and refine the form.

A Bell-Metal Cup

At Nabadwip, wonderfully thin-walled, elegantly shaped cups (*sada bati*) are wrought from solid ingots of bell metal cast by the artisans themselves (nos. 34, 35). Mukherjee writes that although Nabadwip has many refugee artisans from Bangladesh, these are made by its own traditional artisans. Small though they are, these cups require teamwork. After the ingot has been removed from its open mold, three hammermen sit in a circle to hammer it flat on an anvil, taking turns blow by blow. The master holds the piece with forceps, shifting it so that the blows fall uniformly. At a certain point the metal must be reheated so that it will not become brittle from hammering.

When flat enough, eight to ten of the rounds are gathered up and hammered in a pile until they reach a diameter of about 5½″.

Each small plate is then cut with scissors to a perfect circle. A pile of perhaps a dozen are hammered together on a concave anvil to give them their cupped shape. The top eight become most curved, the bottom three are removed and turned into wider mouthed bowls. The bottoms are hammered flat, and the elegant profile is formed by the master on shaped anvils, first in fours and then two at a time. Because the cups are so thin, they can be worked together in this manner.

The cups are cleaned up with a file and, on the inside, a curved steel scraper until they shine. They are attached with resin to a hand-turned lathe for a final polishing. For an even finer finish, the customer can have them machine polished in a shop.

A Water Jar

(Cf. nos. 30 and 31) Bali-Dewanganj is near Arambagh in the Hooghly district, where, probably not coincidentally, superior clays are available for mold making. The town has long been a metalworking center of renown; the artisans, Karmakar by caste and Rauth by surname, say they have always lived there. Their kin and marriage ties extend to Midnapur, Bankura, Burdwan, and Purulia.

The Bali-Dewanganj water-pot described by Mukherjee is a well-known item widely used in West Bengal. It is cast in two halves, then hammered and soldered together at the middle. The mold into which the metal will be poured is formed from a copper or bronze water-pot used as a pattern. In order to capture the curve of the neck and rim and the bulge of the body, the mold is made in three sections, a bowl-shaped bottom, a top shoulder, and a mouth (these last two will be cast as one unit). Each mold has an interior and exterior component, and when

they are joined together, the metal will be poured into the space between the two.

Funnel-necked clay crucibles are filled with metal pieces and joined directly to the molds with more clay. The mold and crucible unit are packed around with burning coals in the furnace's firing chamber, a cylindrical hole. When the metal is molten, the unit is removed, shaken, and turned upside down so that the metal can pour down through the neck of the crucible into the mold. When cool, the molds must be broken to remove the cast pieces; water jars are nevertheless standard in shape and size because the mold has been made from a pattern.

The two pieces of the jar, top and bottom, are then joined at the middle, inverted on a round-ended stake for an anvil, and hammered around the seam until the grip is actually watertight. The joint is also soldered with a tin-brass with a small soldering furnace. The soldering iron presses the solder onto the join.

The jar is then scraped and polished on a lathe, and lines are incised on the surface. The final polishing materials are hair and oil, jute bags, and lastly, cow-dung ash.

A Solid Cast Image

(Cf. nos. 5 and 6) In the metalworking center of Natunbazar, Calcutta, in Sett Magan Lane, Mukherjee found solid and hollow-cast images of "classical" type being made of brass and other alloys.

In this workshop, the pattern from which the molds are made is an unbaked clay image made by the artisan who will cast it in metal. (Wooden or stone images are also sometimes used, to different effect.) To make the pattern, a lotus base is prepared of clay and rice husk. An armature of wire and bamboo is pushed into the base and a clay and rice-husk torso built up over it and wrapped in clay-coated cloth. The head is made separately of sandy clay mixed with fine clay, pressed into a standard mold. After drying and re-touching with a bamboo knife, the head is attached to the torso. The whole pattern is then left to dry before receiving a final detailing with the bamboo knife.

For the mold, a mix of sandy clay, fine clay, and chopped jute is prepared. The pattern is smeared with mustard oil and a dusting of ash, and then covered over with the mold preparation. Each section of the mold is reinforced with shaped iron rods, and a second coat of clay applied. The mold is constructed so that it can be tapped apart into sections: a foot-high figure requires separate sections for the back half, top to bottom, the front from the waist up, the front from the waist down, and the base, the right hand and forearm, and the left hand and forearm. The sections are pulled away from the pattern, reassembled into a hollow mold, wired, and covered thickly with clay. The metal will be poured into a hole prepared earlier in the bottom of the base (a second hole will allow gasses to escape).

Although Mukherjee does not describe the casting process, the metal presumably is melted in a separate crucible and poured into the mold. The furnace is a brick-lined pit with a grate of iron rods. The metal image must be broken out of the mold, but the pattern can be repaired if necessary and reused.

When a patron requests "eight-metal" rather than brass, an alloy of brass, lead, iron and zinc is prepared, perhaps with a small amount of gold and silver in the form of a small ball sealed separately inside the image.

A Rice Measuring Bowl (Cf. Cat. no. 39, and for other examples of this type of work, nos. 59 to 63) At the other end of the so-called folk-urban continuum, we find a *dokra* rice measuring bowl made by the Malhar of Dariapur, described in some detail above. *Dokra* work is an unusual

kind of *cire perdue* or lost wax casting in which the model is made of wax or resin threads wrapped over a clay core. It is "hollow cast," that is, it has a shell of metal over an internal clay core which may or may not be removed after firing.

To make a bowl, an undecorated, bowl-shaped clay core is filed smooth, calibrated to size, and dried in the sun. Tapes and threads of warm *sal* tree resin mixed with mustard oil are applied to the outside of the core. Every design detail in the final cast piece must be present on the resin model, for there is no further finishing of the piece after casting. These threads are clearly visible in the objects on display.

The resin-covered core is covered with several layers of clay slip mixed with ash. The slip must be both fine and porous so that it faithfully renders the details of the design while allowing burnt resin to vaporize through the mold's walls. Thicker layers of clay are added, including the flaring neck to which the brass-filled crucible will be attached. The unit is baked to vaporize the resin and melt the metal. As with the Bali-Dewanganj jar, the mold is pulled out of the fire, tipped to let the metal flow into the mold, and cooled. The bowl is broken out of the mold, the core chipped away from the inside, and the whole wire brushed and filed to clean and burnish it.

From the artisan's hand, the finished pieces go out to the purchaser: housewife, wedding guest, temple donor. Their making in one sense is complete only when they take their place in the new owner's life, which frequently means a life of ritual. Thus the image is finished not when it leaves the hand of the artisan to be bought, but when it is entered by the deity. It will acquire a new history, some of which can be read in the wear it incurs and the traces of the sacred and everyday materials with which it was filled or cov-

ered. It may finally be discarded. Or, in the case of the objects here on display, it may be removed from its round of daily and ritual life to be become part of an exhibition at a public museum. From here it enters the lives of the audience. At the New-ark Museum, this audience is American and Bengali alike; both are invited to participate in the daily life and ritual of Bengal.

NOTES

1. Anyone who studies traditional metalworking in India (or elsewhere) owes a great debt to Meera Mukherjee and Ruth Reeves and their monographs on metalworking in India: Meera Mukherjee, *Metalcraftsmen of India* (Calcutta: Anthropological Survey of India, 1978) and Ruth Reeves, *Cire Perdue Casting in India* (New Delhi: Crafts Museum, 1962).

2. T. N. Mukharji, "A Monograph on the Brass, Bronze, and Copper Manufactures of Bengal," in *Art in Industry Through the Ages* (New Delhi: Navrang, 1976 [1895 or 1897]), p. 301.

3. This description is drawn primarily from my own fieldwork and from the "Handicrafts Survey Monograph on Dokra Artisans of Dariapur (Burdwan)," *Census of India 1961, West Bengal and Sikkim,* Vol. XVI, VII-A, no. 4 (Delhi: Manager of Publications, Government of India, 1973).

4. See Meera Mukherjee, "Metalcraftsmen, Their Work and Environment," *Journal of the Indian Anthropological Society* 19, no. 1 (1984): 66–79, for a brief survey and sensitive analysis of the current state of metal workers in eastern India, including West Bengal.

5. Michael W. Meister, "Preface," in *Making Things in South Asia: The Role of the Artist and Craftsman,* edited by Michael W. Meister (Philadelphia: Department of South Asia Regional Studies, 1988), p. x.

6. R. C. Agrawala and Vijay Kumar, "Ganeshwar-Jodhpura Culture: New Traits in India Archaeology," in *Harappan Civilization,* edited by Gregory L. Possehl (New Delhi: Oxford & IBH Publishing Co., 1982), pp. 125–134.

7. P. T. Craddock et al., "The Production of Lead, Silver and Zinc in Early India," in *Old World Metallurgy,* edited by A. Hauptmann, E. Pernicka, and G. A. Wagner (Bochum: Deutschen Bergbau-Museums, 1989), pp. 61, 66.

8. Reeves quotes L. S. Neelankantan to the effect that copper (and its alloys) was chosen for its ability to transfer to the image the stored energy, the light and fire, of the temple's inner shrine and carry it to devotees outside. For that reason it was and is preferred even over gold and silver for making images. Ruth Reeves, *Cire Perdue Casting in India* (New Delhi: Crafts Museum, 1962), p. 108.

9. Meera Mukherjee, *Metalcraftsmen of India* (Calcutta: Anthropological Survey of India, 1978), pp. 295–300.

10. Ibid., pp. 308–314.

11. Ibid., pp. 300–307.

12. Ibid., pp. 314–319.

13. Lee Horne, "Itinerant Brasscasters of Eastern India," in *Living Traditions: Studies in the Ethnoarchaeology of South Asia,* edited by Bridget Allchin (New Delhi: Oxford & IBH Publishing Co., 1994), pp. 271–273.

CATALOGUE

Mango-Shaped Container
Catalogue no. 63

A priest wakes up images of Krishna and Radha asleep in a wooden home shrine. Flanking the central shrine are smaller metal shrines containing Nadugopala and a shalagrama stone.

A priest prepares one of several altars as part of a wedding ceremony assisted by the bride's father.

Shrines

When a Bengali family moves into a new home, a primary concern is to locate a suitable space for the household's gods. Images are usually placed in a small altar in a clean area of the house. This may be a corner of the kitchen or a small prayer room. In more affluent homes a separate room may be constructed with a sanctum, an area to accomodate devotees, and spaces for storing supplies and to prepare offerings. If sufficient space is not available for such a shrine, a low wooden platform on the floor or a shelf on the wall can be used to set up the altar. Once the gods are given their place, they are invoked to bless the family's new home.

In addition to these permanent metal or wooden shrines that are the focus for daily worship, temporary shrines may be set up in various parts of the house for special ceremonies. Auspicious objects such as a young banana plant, a cluster of mango leaves, or a water-pot may be used to define these spaces, and to give protection by warding off evil spirits. The seat of the deity is usually marked by symbolic designs made of rice paste and by objects used to serve the deity. An icon of the deity is then installed at this specially marked location for use during the ceremony.

Temporary shrines are constructed also for public festivals, when large images of straw, mud, and terracotta are set up for community worship. These images are immersed in some body of water—a river, lake, or the ocean—at the end of the festival period and the temporary shrine is dismantled. If temples (pp. 26, 78) act as the residence of deities—their palaces on earth—they also represent and enclose the altar for human sacrifice. A home shrine offers divinity a shelter within the household and the family a doorway to the divine.

1

42

2

1. Shrine with Images of Krishna and Radha

Brass/ Height: 38″
Eighteenth-nineteenth century
Gift of Dr. and Mrs. Richard J. Nalin, 1987
and 1988   88.480, 87.186, 87.187

2. Shrine

Brass/ Height: 17½″
Eighteenth-nineteenth century
Gift of Dr. and Mrs. Richard J. Nalin, 1987
and 1988   88.481

As do temples, home shrines house and protect the physical bodies of the gods. Some
shrines have metal deity images inside them
as in no. 1, while others are purchased
empty and in these may be placed a variety
of metal images, framed photographs, or implements.[1] Shrines also serve as thrones for
the gods and stand on four legs that take the
form of lion's claws, as do the lion-clawed
legs of thrones for kings. A prototype exists
in the National Museum, Dhaka.

1. Mallebrein (1993), pp. 139, 173.

*A wooden home shrine with its curtain open to display
metal implements and clay deity images.*

A woman dresses a brass image of Radha.

A priest smears fragrant sandalwood paste on his palm, which he will use to create ornamental patterns on the forehead of each deity.

A home altar can combine metal images and calendar photographs of a wide range of deities (here including Shiva, Kali, Chandi, Lakshmi, Hanuman, Krishna, and Radha).

Images for Worship

Not only are the gods universal and transcendent, but also local and immanent in a variety of forms to receive the worship of their devotees. Universal deities are present in temples; immanent and local in home and village shrines for daily worship. Divinity may also manifest itself in rocks, under trees, or in natural sites such as caves, glaciers, and river banks, which may become places of pilgrimages. The gods can assume a human shape through images or make themselves accessible through the bodies of saints and spiritual teachers.

In the home, family members develop a highly personal and intimate relationship with the localized manifestations of transcendent deities in the shrine. The family's gods are present in the shrine in a variety of vessels: given body by metal, stone, or clay images (nos. 3,4); calendar photographs and paintings; patterns on the floor; water-pots (no. 31); or naturally occurring objects such as plants or ammonite fossils (*shalagrama*) (no. 16). Such objects are infused with the presence of the deity through the worshiper's devotion. Images come alive only through this ritual use.

In the home, a wide range of objects function equally as containers of the divine substance and as vehicles through which the gods enter the shrine and bless the household. From the viewpoint of function, an earthen pot or a calendar painting is no less significant than is a metal icon as a vessel for the deity. The anthropomorphic and the more abstract manifestations of divinity receive equal attention and care from the devotee. It is not uncommon to see all of these objects placed next to each other. A calendar picture may be awakened, bathed, dressed, garlanded, decorated with sandalwood and sindoor paste, and fed in the same way as can a metal icon, water-pot, or jar of rice. Transcendent deities have been made present in each of these by the rituals performed.

In contrast to the formal hierarchy of images in a temple, the great flexibility by which the family can determine what is suitable for worship in the home may be due in part to the emphasis on establishing a personal and initimate relationship with the gods.

3. *Durga Mahishamardini*

Copper Alloy/ Height: 9½″
Fifteenth-sixteenth century; purchased from
Chittagong
Gift of Dr. David R. Nalin, 1988   88.297

4. *Durga Mahishamardini*

Brass, with cloth garments/ Height: 21″
Eighteenth-nineteenth century
Gift of Dr. and Mrs. Richard J. Nalin, 1988
88.483

Both images depict Durga slaying Mahisha,
the demon who takes a buffalo's form. She is
poised with one foot on the back of her lion.
Her ten hands clasp powerful weapons. The
demon is transforming himself into a human
being as Durga and her lion attack him. In
these images, a human head is emerging
from the buffalo's body.

Both images are mounted on rectangular
pedestals that also support the figures of
Durga's four children: Ganesa, to her right,
with an elephant's trunk; Lakshmi, above,
with a lotus bud in her hand; Saraswati to
Durga's left; and Kartikeya, the battle chief
with his sword and shield, below.

Although the iconography of these two
images is quite similar, ritually they have
quite different meanings. An old and worn
image is usually not kept in a shrine or worshiped as the goddess. The image is usually
removed from the shrine and replaced by a
new, shiny, metal image or a freshly painted
one. The life of the deity is then renewed in
this newly installed image.

An image in good physical condition is
considered suitable to be dressed, garlanded,
and given jewelry and cosmetics. Bathing
and dressing the bodies of the gods is a major part of the preparation for worship. Only
when they have received this service do the
gods grant their benediction.

5

5. *Krishna and Radha*

Brass/ Heights: 7½", 5½"
Eighteenth century
Gift of Dr. and Mrs. Richard J. Nalin, 1988
88.494, 88.495

Krishna is the eighth incarnation of Vishnu,
and Radha, his lover, is usually identified
with Vishnu's consort, Lakshmi. Krishna is
the divine flute player, and he is shown
dancing to the music of his flute.[1] Radha
holds a lotus bud as if in offering to Krishna's
divine form. Radha and Krishna are the most
important deities of Bengali Vaishnavism.
Their worship in home shrines continues to
be very popular today.

1. Cf. no. 5 with Skelton and Francis (1979), p. 24 and
no. 6 with Davidson (1968), p. 69, fig. 94.

6. *Krishna*

Brass/ Height: 11"
Sixteenth-seventeenth century
Gift of Dr. and Mrs. Richard J. Nalin, 1988
88.493

This particularly ornate image of Krishna
represents him wearing a short *dhoti* with a
floral pattern, an elaborate waistband, and
pleats. He is further adorned with star-
shaped earrings, necklaces, anklets and
bracelets. He wears wooden sandals called
khorom on his feet. By comparison, no. 7 is
less ornate.

6

7. *Krishna as Venu Gopala*

Brass/ Height: 10″
Seventeenth-eighteenth century
Gift of Dr. David R. Nalin, 1988   88.370

8. *Krishna as Nadu Gopala*

Brass/ Height: 4¼″
Nineteenth century
Gift of Dr. David R. Nalin, 1988   88.374

The worship of Krishna is of great importance to Vaishnavism in Bengal. The most intimate relationship that the devotee may have with the deity is that of a lover, as Radha was to Krishna. Next in importance to that union is the love of a mother for her son, where the worshiper treats Krishna as if he were her son. In these human forms, the powerful god becomes accessible to the devotee. The mythology of Krishna provides engaging stories about various stages of his growing up that might strike a chord of remembrance of similar experiences in his worshipers.

These two brass images of Krishna depict aspects of the deity that are very popular for worship in the intimate setting of the home. Krishna, the divine flute player, moves his body to the music of his flute, which is now missing.[1] As an infant, he is depicted crawling, with stolen sweetmeats clasped in his hand. According to the Bengali version of the legend, baby Krishna stole sweets from his mother's kitchen, rather than butter as elsewhere in India, and was caught as he crawled away.[2]

1. Cf. Skelton and Francis (1979), p. 24.
2. Cf. Bussabarger and Robins (1968), p. 111.

7

8

9

10

9. *Durga Mahishamardini*

Painted Porcelain/ Height: 9″
Nineteenth century
Gift of Dr. and Mrs. Richard J. Nalin, 1988
88.521

This image of Durga as slayer of Mahisha, the buffalo demon, is remarkable for the material from which it is made. Such European manufacture may have been introduced into Bengal in the nineteenth century, and must have become quite popular in middle-class homes for its luster and beauty. Durga stands with one foot on the back of her lion and the other on the demon, surrounded by her four children. The frame and presentation of this image closely resembles an ivory plaque exhibited at the Great Exhibition of 1851 (London), and this object may represent an inexpensive substitute for that much more expensive material.[1]

1. See Skelton and Francis (1979), p. 75, fig. 232.

10. *Krishna and Radha*

Painted Porcelain/ Height: 9¾″
Nineteenth-twentieth century
Gift of Dr. and Mrs. Richard J. Nalin, 1988
88.522

Krishna in this porcelain image resembles Venugopala in the way he stands with one foot over the other (cf. nos. 5, 7). Quite distinct from the more hieratic images of these deities, these figures seem to have been conceived in European terms. Unlike the previous images (no. 5), they here share a single pedestal and tenderly clasp each other. Contact with European sculpture is also evident in their clothing, especially the swirling cloaks, and the knot of Krishna's *dhoti*. Radha's costume almost takes on qualities of the many marble images in Queen Victoria's India.

11

11. Gajalakshmi

Bronze/ Height: 5½″
Nineteenth-twentieth century
Gift of Dr. David R. Nalin, 1988   88.387

Gajalakshmi, as a particular aspect of the
goddess Lakshmi, is shown flanked by elephants who bathe her with water. As the
goddess of fertility and motherhood, she is
worshiped in rural homes by women who
want to be blessed with healthy children.

In this image, the goddess is represented
in a folk idiom which is unusual in that it depicts Lakshmi supporting the elephants that
constitute the heads of the maces that she
carries.[1] Their trunks unite above her, creating a frame for the image. The flower-shaped
finial is intended to hold incense.

1. Cf. the figure of the goddess in Dallapiccola (1984),
fig. 123.

12. *Vishnu with Consorts*

Copper/ Height: 3¾″
Twelfth century
Gift of Dr. David R. Nalin, 1988   88.390

This classical "bronze" of the Pala-Sena period depicts Vishnu with his consorts Sri and
Saraswati, each on their separate lotus pedestals.[1] Vishnu wears a tall, conical headdress
and holds the traditional emblems in his four
hands—discus, conch shell, lotus, and mace.
Sri holds a lotus and Saraswati a musical in-
strument called *veena*. At the center of the
stepped pedestal supporting these three figures is Garuda, the half-bird half-man emblem of Vishnu, easily recognized by his
protruding beak and folded wings.

1. Cf. Casey (1985), pp. 72–73, figs. 44, 45.

12

13. *Uma Maheshvara*

Copper Alloy/ Height: 4″
Tenth century
Gift of Dr. David R. Nalin, 1989   89.141

Uma and Maheshvara, that is Shiva and his
bride Parvati, are the paradigmatic husband-
and-wife team of the Hindu pantheon.[1] He is
the lord of the universe, and in particular, of
death and destruction. His trident is shown
wrapped by a snake and ornamented with a
skull. Through the power of his third eye
and his meditation, Maheshvara sets entire
worlds ablaze at the end of cosmic time cycles. Uma is the beautiful young daughter of
the Himalayan mountains. Here they are
shown in dalliance in his palace on Mount
Kailasha.

Today, it is believed that when Maheshvara is angry he wreaks havoc on the world,
but when appeased and calmed, he is the
model husband. Young Bengali girls are
taught to pour water over images of Maheshvara to cool his anger, to observe fasts to win
his favor, and to dedicate themselves to his
service in order to win a husband who meets
Maheshvara's ideal. They are also taught to
model themselves after Uma, who served
Maheshvara faithfully and suffered his rages
patiently.

1. Published in Casey (1985), p. 37, fig. 14.

13

14

14. Lakshmi

Brass/Metal/ Height: 7¼″
Twentieth century
Gift of Mr. and Mrs. Jay Dehejia, 1986
86.327

This "folk" image of the goddess Lakshmi, made by the wax-wire process, shows her riding on her traditional vehicle, a giant owl. Behind, a spiky aureole surrounds her.[1] Such an image may have been commissioned by rural housewives from itinerant artisans.[2] These women usually provide the metal scraps as this lowers the cost of the image.

According to the *Matsya Purana,* Lakshmi arose from the primordial ocean when it was churned for ambrosia, and she was claimed by Vishnu as his consort. Although she is associated with Vishnu, in Bengal she is venerated in her own right as the goddess of the harvest and prosperity. Her most important festival occurs on the night of the harvest moon, when she is invoked to bless the newly harvested rice crop. She is worshiped in temporary street pavilions, in temples as well as in home shrines at this time. Temporary shrines are set up in the home with an image of Lakshmi, a pot of rice, and rice-paste patterns of her footprints on the floor.

Lakshmi is also the goddess who presides over women and the home. They pray to her for peace and prosperity, thrift and order. The good housewife is called *lakshmi,* the benevolent goddess of the home, and a well-mannered, disciplined daughter is also called *lakshmi.*

In contrast to a "classical" image such as that of Uma and Maheshvara (no. 13), this image represents a traditional art form known as *dokra,* practiced by specialized communities of craftsmen such as the Malhar. It is cast by a particular variety of the "lost-wax" process by which threads of resin wrapped around a clay core are melted out by the entry of liquified metal, either brass or cheaper scrap metal.

1. For a similar frame, see Dallapiccola (1984), p. 114.
2. Ghose (1981), pp. 61–2.

15

15. *Nine Goddesses in a Lotus*

Copper/ Height: 4¾"
Sixteenth century; Nepal
Gift of Dr. and Mrs. Richard J. Nalin, 1990
90.400

Collapsible shrines offer worshipers an intimate way of relating to the deity. This copper lotus appears to rise out of the water, with its square support decorated by waves. The lotus had eight petals and on each sits a female deity with distinctive attributes and animal vehicles. They represent nine aspects of Durga: Maheshvari, the power of Shiva; Varahi, consort of the boar incarnation of Vishnu; Vaishnavi, the female aspect of Vishnu; Indrani, the feminine power of Indra on an elephant; Camunda, a powerful and warlike aspect of Durga; Narasimhi, the female aspect of the incarnation of Vishnu as man-lion; Kaumari, the power of Kartikeya on his peacock; and (missing) Brahmani, the female aspect of Brahma. The center of the flower once supported a figure of Durga.

Images such as this one, purchased in Nepal, were often brought by travelers and used in home shrines in eastern India. Worship of Durga as the personification of universal energy became widespread in Bengal between the eleventh and twelfth centuries, and from this time onward her complex representations became very popular. Pala-period lotus *mandalas* representing Vishnu's incarnations, sets of goddesses, and Buddhist deities are well known.[1]

1. See N. R. Ray (1986), fig. 281, and Huntington (1984), fig. 196.

Plates with flowers and sweets, vessels with water, a handbell, conch shell, and a shalagrama *stand are laid out on painted rice-paste patterns for the worship of Vishnu. In the far background are a clay plate with coconut husk and a reed fan for burning camphor.*

A priest rings a bell and waves a lighted lamp before the deity while performing the final ritual of arati *at the end of the day.*

Implements of Ritual

Daily worship consists of a sequence of rituals that involve action, gestures, words, and objects used to bring together the devotee and the gods. Objects derived from everyday life are invested with sacred meaning when used in the service of the deity. Morning *puja* is initiated with the blowing of the conch shell, welcoming the deity to the prayer room, to proclaim the presence of the deity in the image, and to beckon members of the household.

The water-pot is one of the most important vessels used in daily worship. The pot is said to contain silt and water from the Ganges, the holiest river of northern India. In practice, however, this water may be obtained from a local pond, river, or tank. The pot gives form to the deity—the water and earth in the pot are the elements of the divine as well as of the human body. During worship, the water-pot serves as a conduit through which divine substance is transmitted into an image or the pot itself contains certain deities. The water-pot is ritually "dressed" and marked with a red or white pattern at its widest part. The neck is lined with mango leaves and a banana or coconut is often placed on top.

Water for ritual oblation is carried in smaller receptacles during the course of the ritual. Some of these are in the shape of the *yoni*, which represents female generative power (no. 21).

Food and other auspicious items are offered to the deity on large brass, copper, or stone platters, just as food might be served to a visitor. Items placed on the platter must be suitable for an offering to the gods. These offerings may include substances of daily use such as mustard oil mixed with turmeric, unhusked rice grains, clarified butter, and curd. Vermilion powder, signifying marriage and mud, symbolizing the River Ganga may also be offered. Women choose beautiful gifts such as sandalwood paste, flowers, and leaves for the goddesses.

Objects used for *arati*, the final ritual in the evening are a small hand-held lamp, a censer for camphor, and another for incense (nos. 25, 28; 22; 26). The worshiper captures the heat of the lamp in the palm of the hand as a blessing from the deity.

Many of these rituals parallel domestic rituals and the vessels and substances are the same as those used in the kitchen. In the home, lighting of a lamp at dusk acquires special meaning when it is lit near the basil plant in the garden. The lamp not only lights up the house but also lights up the path of the gods as they pass by on their heavenly journeys. The sacredness of the lamp is renewed each time the act of lighting is performed. *Ghee* and curd are as important for cooking as in ritual and poured water as suggestive of the Ganga in the kitchen as in the shrine.

Personal interaction with the deities in a household's daily routine suggests that there are few divisions between worship and daily activity. All activity in the home is imbued by worship. From the morning *puja* when the deities are awakened they are present in the activities of the home. At the evening *arati* they fall asleep, only to be awakened again the next morning by the family's use of implements of ritual.

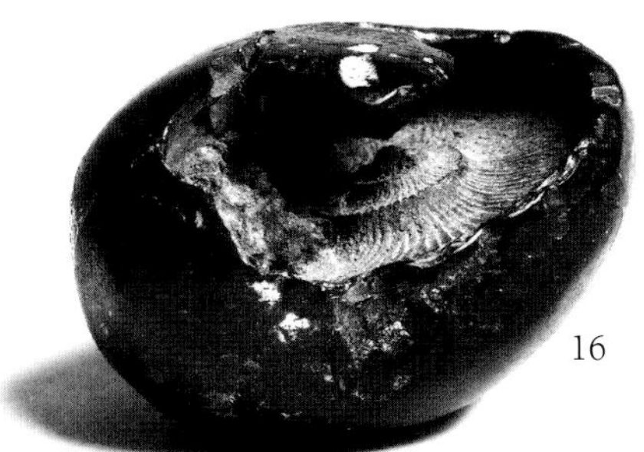

16

16. *Shalagrama*

Ammonite Fossil/ Length: 2½″
Gift of Dr. David R. Nalin, 1988   88.329

This black stone is worshiped as a form of
Vishnu, the god who preserves the cosmic
order.[1] These stones are considered highly
potent since they are naturally occurring
manifestations of Vishnu and one of the few
forms of divinity that cannot be approached
directly by women. Brahmin priests are usually in possession of the stones, which they
carry to the homes where they perform a
ceremony, placing the stone on a stand
owned by the host family (see no. 17). The
stone is then treated just as are the metal images of the god: it is bathed, garlanded, and
offered food.

   This stone was found in a group with
other similar stones and a Pala-period
Vishnu image.

1. See Maxwell, *In the Image of Man* (1982), p. 95,
figs. 1–2.

17. *Shalagrama Stand*

Bronze/ Height: 23¼″
Eighteenth century
Gift of Dr. and Mrs. Richard J. Nalin, 1988
88.482

These stands support black ammonite fossils
(no. 16) that are worshiped as Vishnu. They
act as the equivalent of the lotus throne at
the base of metal anthropomorphic images
(no. 12), or the shrines in which gods reside
(no. 1). This stand takes the form of a fantas-
tic animal, lotus vine, and flower.[1]

1. See Kramrisch (1968), p. 109, fig. 317.

17

18. Vishnu and Lakshmi

Brass/ Heights: 15½″, 13½″
Nineteenth-twentieth century
Gift of Dr. and Mrs. Richard J. Nalin, 1988
88.531, 88.532

Such figures of Vishnu and his consort are quite distinct from "classical" Pala representations of the same deities (see no. 12). Here the gods are conceived as human figures, with contemporary clothing, jewelry, and facial features. Lakshmi wears her *sari* in a style common even today. Neither stands on a lotus base. These images reflect contact with Western traditions, using human models for the representation of divinities. The figures may have been curios of the colonial period or attending objects in a home shrine.

19

19. Saturn, One of the Nine Planets

Copper/ Height: 3¾"
Nineteenth-twentieth century
Gift of Dr. David R. Nalin, 1988   88.420

Saturn is identified by the water-pot in his
hand and the tortoise on which he stands.
The nine planets are worshiped for rain,
peace and prosperity, long life and nourishment, and for revenge.[1] Such an image may
have been worshiped in its own right or used
as an attendant in a home shrine.

1. Banerjea (1941), p. 443.

20. Saint

Brass/ Height: 10¼"
Nineteenth-twentieth century
Gift of Dr. and Mrs. Richard J. Nalin, 1988
88.506

This image depicts a saint with the character-
istic hand gestures of a wandering holy man,
who sings praises to the gods, while cupping
his ear to hear his own song. Ecstatic song
and dance as expressions of devotion were
encouraged by, for example, Caitanya, the
saint who led the Bengali Vaishnava movement in the sixteenth century. The word *gu-
rudaya* meaning "blessing of the saint" is incised in Bengali script on the saint's garment.
In a home shrine, it is customary to worship
images of spiritual leaders along with those
of the gods.

20

21

21. Water Vessel

Copper/ Length: 18¼″
Nineteenth-twentieth century
Gift of Dr. and Mrs. Richard J. Nalin, 1988
88.549

These sinuous vessels are used exclusively to
hold holy water during worship. The worshiper dips flowers, leaves, and other items
into this water to purify them before offering
them to the gods. The vessel is usually ac-
companied by a small copper ladle of the
same shape to pour water on the metal images when bathing the gods. The shape of
the vessel is a conventional representation of
the womb and is associated with fertility.
The large size of this particular vessel suggests that it was used in a temple rather than
in a home shrine.

22

22. *Camphor Censer*

Brass/ Width: 19″
Nineteenth-twentieth century
Gift of Dr. David R. Nalin, 1988   88.300

Camphor is usually burned during evening
worship, as well as at other rituals. The
smoke and scent are considered to be purifying. Layers of burning coals and dried coconut bark serve to ignite the camphor powder
in the censer. A hand fan (no. 47) is then
waved to cool the flames so that the powder
simmers over the smouldering coals for the
entire length of the ritual.

This graceful weighted censer has six legs
and a long chain to suspend it from the
ceiling.

23. *Standing Lamp with Peacocks*

Brass/ Height: 18″
Twentieth century
Gift of Dr. and Mrs. Richard J. Nalin, 1988
88.566

Oil lamps are lighted to provide light in the
evening and to burn flying insects and other
impurities in the air. The flame invokes the
presence of Agni, god of fire, in temple and
home rituals. This standing lamp consists of
a vertical column divided into tiers by five
rings, alternately ornamented as peacocks
with projecting heads and tails. The hollow
receptacle at the top is filled with oil burnt
with a cotton wick. The word *devi* (goddess)
is incised below the lowermost peacock.[1]

1. Cf. *dokra* lamps in Dallapiccola (1984), p. 84,
figs. 274–277.

24. *Hand Bell*

Bronze/ Height: 5¼″
Nineteenth-twentieth century
Gift of Dr. David R. Nalin, 1988   88.412

Hand bells are rung before the image of the
deity. They are held in the left hand while a
lamp is waved in the right hand. This bell
terminates in a figure of Garuda, Vishnu's
vehicle.

23

24

25

25. *Small Lamp with Cobra Hood*

Brass/ Height: 1¾″
Twentieth century
Gift of Dr. David R. Nalin, 1988   88.627

This very small lamp is held in the hand
and waved before the image of the deity to
ward off evil, especially during the ritual
known as *arati*. The flame is protected by a
cobra's hood.

26

26. Incense Holder

Brass/ Height: 7¼″
Eighteenth-nineteenth century
Gift of Dr. and Mrs. Richard J. Nalin, 1988
88.409

This stand holds lighted incense sticks that
are waved before the gods in the shrine.
Similar to the *shalagrama* stand (no. 17), this
holder takes the form of a leogryph and a
vine.

27

27. Hanging Lamp

Brass/ Height: 6¼″, 21½″ with chain
Twentieth century
Gift of Dr. and Mrs. Richard J. Nalin, 1988
88.551

Lamps are suspended from the ceiling by a
hook in front of the home or temple sanctum
and must be lighted each evening. This slen-
der lamp takes the form of a bird.[1] The bird
stands on a flower whose petals are the oil
cups for cotton wicks.

1. Cf. Bussabarger and Robins (1968), p. 82.

28. Lamp

Brass/ Height: 6¼″
Nineteenth-twentieth century
Gift of Dr. and Mrs. Richard J. Nalin, 1988
88.562

This lamp, in the form of a lotus flower, was
held in rituals much as candles were once
carried to bed. A stem rising from a lotus
base supports a ring of tiny cups which ra-
diate from the center like the petals of a
blooming flower. Each receptacle can be
filled with oil to fuel a cotton wick. The
handle takes the form of a vine by which
the lamp can be raised and waved before the
deity during morning and evening worship.
After the fire has been graced by the deity,
the sanctified flame is offered to all the
family members, who receive its warmth in
their palms to receive the blessing.

28

29

29. Manasa Water-Pot

Brass/ Height: 6¾″
Tenth-twelfth century
Gift of Dr. David R. Nalin, 1989   89.142

Plain earthen pots containing holy water are
used today in rural Bengal to worship Manasa, the goddess of snakes. They give a body
to the goddess, whether she is given an image or not. This Pala-period metal water-pot
has been anthropomorphized with three figures on its shoulder. Above the spout and
sheltered by a hood of seven snakes sits
Manasa, fruit in her right hand and a snake
in her left. To her right is her husband Jarat-
karu; on her left is her son Astika. A snake
winds around the belly of the pot below the
figures.[1]

During the monsoon, when floods bring
forth snakes, young girls perform vows for
the welfare and health of their families using
these pots at the center of rituals. In rural
homes, pots are often filled with milk and
kept in the kitchen so that stray snakes can
drink the milk and go away without harming
anybody. The existence of several such metal
pots from the Pala period suggest that the
village practices of today have a long history.

1. Cf. Skelton and Francis (1979), p. 70, fig. 29.
Published in Casey (1985), pp. 38–39, fig. 15.

30

31

30. Small Water-Pot

Brass/ Height: 2¾″
Twentieth century
Gift of Dr. David R. Nalin, 1988   88.322

31. Large Water-Pot

Bell-metal/ Height: 7½″
Nineteenth-twentieth century
Gift of Dr. David R. Nalin, 1988   88.313

Water-pots perform a wide range of functions, both ritually and domestically. Small water-pots are used for washing feet and bathing; larger ones are used to store water for cooking, drinking, or for washing offerings in the home shrine. Water-pots store holy water from the Ganga and the water is used for special rituals.

Such pots, filled with water and earth, are used to give form to goddesses during home rituals. They are decorated with brightly colored patterns made of rice powder, sandalwood, and vermilion; whole fruits such as mangoes, coconuts, and bananas, leaves, and flowers are placed on top, and the pots are garlanded with flowers. Thus, they are transformed into the deity and prepared to receive worship in the same way as are anthropomorphic images.

The donor has identified no. 31 as coming from Dhamrai, near Dhaka.

A stone plate and bowl are filled with cleaned and cut fruits for use in home ritual.

A priest surveys an array of utensils filled with food already offered to the gods and ready for distribution to the family.

Utensils

Food occupies a central place in Bengali homes. Hospitality toward guests, the service of the gods, and the care of family members reiterate the importance of feeding and eating. A sense of ethic prevails in the preparation, distribution, and consumption of food. Feeding others is essentially an offering, an act of generosity and compassion, and feeding oneself an extension of feeding others.

Feeding is a challenging task: the gods must be fed according to prescriptions concerning their tastes; guests have to be offered the very best. Within the family there are rules concerning widows, who are traditionally vegetarian; suitable meals must be prepared for the sick person; pregnant women should eat foods such as ghee, milk, and sweets that will nurture the unborn baby.

Particular rituals require fasting, eating less, or eating different foods from the usual. On the wedding day, the bride is expected to fast. During the twelve days of mourning, the immediate relatives of the deceased eat balls of rice in order to share in the ritual impurity resulting from death. On the first day of the monsoon, kitchen fires are not lit; instead, the family eats leftovers. On the other hand, on festival days, more elaborate meals than usual are prepared.

Kitchen utensils for cutting, cooking, and serving food, containers for the storage of prepared food, and accessory utensils occupy an important place in the home. Further, cooking utensils are associated with natural prosperity, and by ex-tension, with divine and human fertility. Through these associations, utensils for daily cooking share in part the potency and sanctity of divine images and implements for worship.

Cooking utensils are prized possessions. Families accumulate collections of kitchen utensils in various ways. During the first celebratory eating of rice, a baby is presented the first set of personal utensils such as a silver or gold plate, spoon, and glass. During her wedding, a bride brings new sets of kitchenware to the home of the groom. During other auspicious events, other community and caste members bring gifts of utensils. Often these utensils are inscribed with the name of the individual, the event that it commemorates, and the date. In this way, households acquire expensive collections of gold, silver, bronze, brass, copper, and bell-metal utensils for cooking and serving food.

These collections of shining utensils are often displayed on shelves in the kitchen, dining room, and even living room. They are brought out for use during religious rituals and other family festivities.

In recent times, industrially manufactured stainless steel, glass, ceramic, and plastic are gaining popularity for kitchen use as these materials are cheaper, lighter to carry, and easier to clean. However, they are restricted to the kitchen. It is still necessary to use pure metals such as copper, brass, and bronze in the home shrine.

32, 33

32–33. *Plate and Bowl*

Black Stone/ Diameters: 16½″, 13″
Twentieth century
Gift of Dr. and Mrs. Richard J. Nalin, 1988
88.523, 88.525

Such stone implements are used primarily
for religious rituals to offer food to the gods,
for the annual worship of Durga in the fall,
or for wedding rituals. The bowl is filled
with water and placed on the plate to obtain
a reflection of the goddess during Durga
puja. In wedding rituals, when a bride enters
her husband's home, she places her first step
into a bowl of milk, holding rice and a live
fish in her hands as she is embraced by his
family.

   The hard black stone used to fashion these
implements is quarried from the hills of
Gaya district in Bihar, among other places.

34, 35

36

34–35. *Plate and Bowl*

Bell-Metal/ Diameters: 16¾″, 9¾″
Twentieth century
Gift of Dr. and Mrs. Richard J. Nalin, 1988
88.511, 88.526

36. *Tray with Floral Pattern*

Brass/ Diameter: 32″
Nineteenth-twentieth century
Gift of Dr. and Mrs. Richard J. Nalin, 1988
88.547

Such metal utensils are used primarily for
serving food to the family at meal times and
for presenting offerings to the gods during
worship. The large brass tray (no. 36) has a
tree of life with a profusion of flowers and
leaves incised along its rim, which can be
compared with a similar tray in Bussabarger
and Robins (1968), p. 77.

37

37. *Mortar and Pestle*

Brass/ Heights: 3¼″, 8¼″
Twentieth century
Gift of Dr. David R. Nalin, 1988   88.372

The epitome of a domestic utensil, the mortar and pestle are used for grinding roots, leaves, and spices for cooking food for the family. Yet another set of these utensils is reserved for the preparation of offerings for the gods in the home shrine. The mortar and pestle also serve in the iconography of wedding and menstrual rituals as stand-ins for appropriate sexual activity. Incised on this mortar is a row of eight seated figures.

38. *Mold for Making Sweets*

Black Stone/ Diameter: 4¾″
Twentieth century
Gift of Dr. and Mrs. Richard J. Nalin, 1988
88.489

These circular molds are used to impress floral patterns on foods such as sweets or mango strips. Both surfaces are decorated with delicate patterns of flowers, leaves, and vines.[1]

The sweets are made of milk products and sugar, and are sometimes embellished with nuts, raisins, colored rice, or grated coconut. They are rolled into flat shapes and pressed on the mold to decorate their upper surface. These sweets can be offered to the household deity during *puja*.

1. Kramrisch (1968), p. 111, fig. 343.

39. *Rice Measuring Bowl*

Metal/ Height: 3¼″
Twentieth century
Gift of Dr. David R. Nalin, 1988   88.296

Such bowls are used to measure rice for daily cooking. They are made in various sizes, usually fractions of a *sher*, the measure used for grain in Bengal.[1] These bowls are also used to worship Lakshmi, who is embodied as a bowl of rice set at the center of a rice-paste design on the floor. During the wedding ceremony, the groom pours *sindoor* powder from a rice measuring bowl on the head where the bride parts her hair as a sign of her acceptance as his wife.

This bowl is decorated with garlands, fish swimming in water, rows of beads, and a solitary scorpion.

1. Cf. Dallapiccola (1984), p. 76, figs. 224–228.

38

obverse

39

40

40. Cutting Utensil

Iron/ Length: 18¼″
Twentieth century
Gift of Dr. and Mrs. Richard J. Nalin, 1988
88.564

This utensil (*boti*) is used for cutting fruits
and vegetables. The woman usually sits with
one leg on the base of the tool to keep it
steady while she uses both hands to cut the
fruit. The serrated edge at its tip is used to
grate coconut. Larger ones are used to cut
fish. Each household has one for domestic
use and another reserved for cutting the fruit
offered during a religious ritual.

41. Container for Rolled Betel Leaves

Silver/Height: 6½″
Twentieth century
Gift of Dr. and Mrs. Richard J. Nalin, 1988
88.488

42. Automobile-Shaped Container

Brass/ Length: 10½″
Twentieth century
Gift of Dr. and Mrs. Richard J. Nalin, 1988
88.510

Metal containers for betel leaves and nuts
are found in most households. The leaves
are prepared in a variety of ways: they can
be stuffed with cloves, areca nuts, cinnamon,
lime, or fennel seeds, and rolled into a number of shapes.

This automobile-shaped container has a
hinged lid which, when raised, reveals numerous compartments in which various ingredients could be stored. The conception of
a storage vessel in the form of an automobile
for making *pan* (rolled betel leaves) reflects
British rule and the introduction of automo-
biles to replace bullock carts and palanquins.
The more traditional, graceful, tapering container, on the other hand, was used to keep
the rolled betel leaves after they had been
stuffed with the spices.[1]

1. Cf. no. 41 to Bussabarger and Robins (1968), p. 71.

41

42

43

44

43–46. Mats

Cured and Dyed Marantradichotoma Reed
Lengths: 41½″–46″; Widths: 35″–37½″
Twentieth century
Gift of Dr. and Mrs. Richard J. Nalin, 1988
88.542–5

These patterned mats are laid on the floor as seats for people during the meals. They are also used as prayer mats when the family gathers at the shrine. They protect against the cold and damp of the earthen floors of rural homes during the rainy season. Sometimes the mats are spread on the beds during hot summers to keep out the heat. These mats are soft and pliable enough so that even the large ones can be folded up to six times and stored on shelves.

The mats come in a wide variety of materials, sizes, colors, and patterns. Traditionally made in Faridpur and Comilla districts in Bangladesh, they are now also being produced by migrant families in Coochbehar and Nadia districts of West Bengal. They were traditionally made in village homes by both men and women who tear fine strips of dried reed, dye some, and weave patterns into the mats. These examples have floral as well as abstract patterns created by colored strips set against a natural background.[1]

1. See Sirajuddin (1992), p. 20.

45

46

47

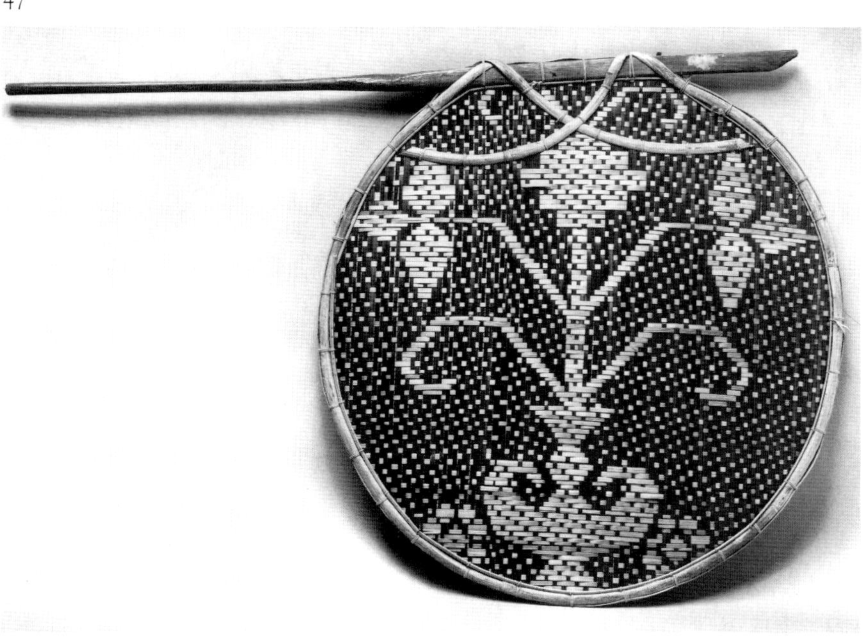

47. Hand Fan

Bamboo Strips/ Length: 17¾″
Twentieth century
Gift of Dr. David R. Nalin, 1988   88.326

Villagers use fans to create a cool breeze in rural homes without electricity during the hot summers. They can also be used to fan deities in a village or home shrine.

Doves, betel leaves, stars, waves, spiders' webs, and huts are popular motifs used to decorate such fans. This particular fan shows a flowering plant rising from a pot, an ancient pattern in India to signify nature's fertility.

Above: A Pala-period stone sculpture of Manjuvajra
shows him sheltered by traditional temple and stupa
forms (collection of David R. Nalin).

Page 26: The Keshta Raya Temple in Bishnupur shows
a form of late medieval brick temple type that
developed in Bengal following vernacular village
forms.

Left: A roadside shrine in east Bengal has absorbed
and co-opted some European form.

Architecture and Ornament

Traditional temples in Bengal took the curvilinear form common throughout northern India. In the late Mughal period, however, Bengal developed a brick temple type (p. 26), covered with carved brick narrative panels, based on earlier vernacular forms. In villages, with patronage from powerful Hindu landholders, painted wooden shrines (nos. 49–51) were set up for home use. Roadside shrines continue to be constructed, sometimes with European or modern elements incorporated into their design.

Many of the traditional arts and crafts of rural Bengal were primarily intended to decorate and embellish the homes. Such crafts include stitching rags into quilts, painting clay covers for jars and pots, weaving bamboo strips into mats, molding clay into toys, and drawing designs with rice paste on the floor. Some of these are leisure activities for women, while others are closely regulated by use in cycles of ritual. For the worship of Lakshmi, for example, women paint the lids of rice jars that they hang on the walls as auspicious ornaments (nos. 56, 57, 58). In Bengal, the ancestral home gives a person his or her identity, and it is not unusual that four to five generations live under the same roof. Consequently, this space must be marked and protected. Objects used in religious rituals and then as decoration act as amulets to ward off evil and attract the gods. Votive objects such as clay figurines of mother goddesses worshiped in the home shrine can be re-used in this way.

The ultimate "ornament" is the shrine itself, the house of the gods; but the lintels, brackets, and door jambs made for it expand and improve on those made for the home itself, as the food for the gods improves on that made daily in the kitchen. The home itself is a shrine; the earth an altar; and worshipers the sacrifice.

48

50

51

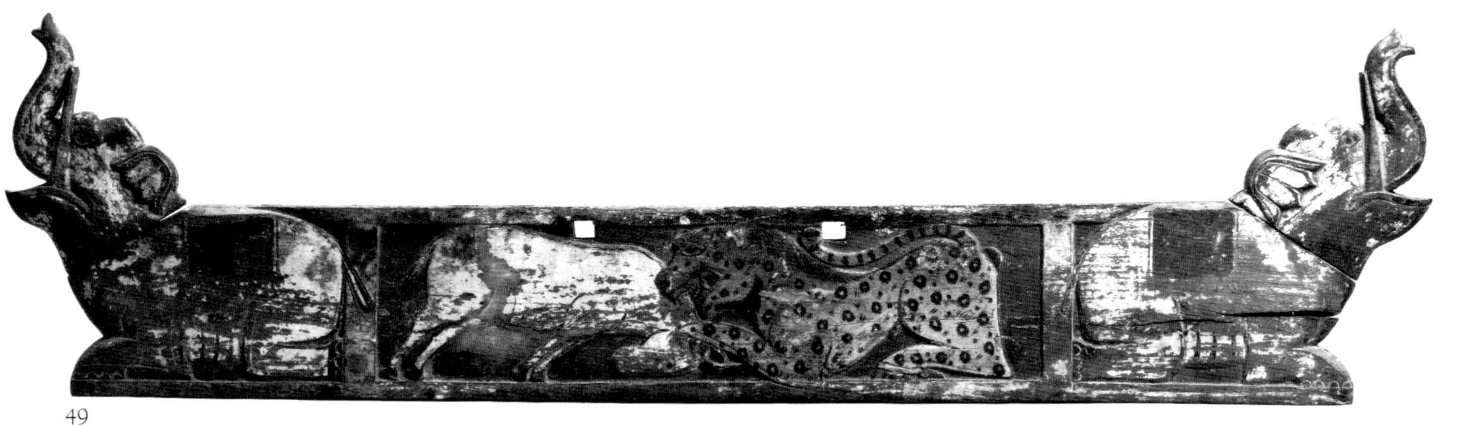

49

48–49. Lintels

Painted Wood/ Lengths: 68″, 66″
Nineteenth-twentieth century
Gift of Dr. and Mrs. Richard J. Nalin, 1988
88.519, 88.520

These lintels, two jambs, a female figure, and
two small panels of Vaishnava avatars (nos.
50, 51) once formed part of a village shrine
in the Dhaka region.

No. 48 has side extensions depicting *mak-aras*—mythical beasts with elephant trunks
and a crocodile's scaly body. Such auspicious
animals guard a shrine, proclaim the deity,
and represent aspects of nature's fertility.[1]
The central part of the beam shows a floral
canopy framing two scenes that represent
contrasting erotic and ascetic themes. On the
left, Rama and Sita embrace each other. The
meditating figure in yogic pose on the right
is Balarama, an avatar of Vishnu, carrying a
plough. The central canopy suggests that the
lintel framed the front entrance of the
wooden shrine.

No. 49 has extensions depicting elephants.
The lintel shows a leopard biting the neck of
a buffalo.

1. See Datta (1990), pp. 62–66.

50. Wood Panel with Figure of Matsya (Fish)

Painted Wood/ Height: 12″
Nineteenth-twentieth century
Gift of Saul and Hilda Mehlman, 1985
85.505B

51. Wood Panel with Figure of Kurma (Tortoise)

Painted Wood/ Height: 12″
Nineteenth-twentieth century
Gift of Saul and Hilda Mehlman, 1985
85.505A

These pieces formed part of a decorative
doorjamb for the same Vaishnava shrine as
the two lintels (nos. 48 and 49). They depict
incarnations of Vishnu—the fish (*matsya*)
and tortoise (*kurma*).

Similar wooden shrine pieces exist in the
National Museum, Dhaka, particularly a
doorjamb from a landholder's house in
Faridpur.

52–53. *Wood Panels with Figures*

Painted Wood/ Heights: 9″, 10¾″
Nineteenth-twentieth century
Gift of Dr. and Mrs. Richard J. Nalin, 1988
88.513, 88.514

These two panels belonged to the door of a wooden home shrine or temple. The upper register (no. 52) illustrates a scene from the epic *Ramayana*, which describes the life and exploits of Rama, the incarnation of Vishnu. Here Rama is shown seated on a lotus throne with a hand raised to bless and acknowledge Hanuman, the monkey king who helped him during his difficulties in the forest. Hanuman is shown with his hands folded in obeisance.

The lower register (no. 53) depicts a saintly figure, who is six-armed. Two of these arms carry a water-pot and a staff, while two other arms lift a flute to the saint's lips, and a final set of arms are raised as if in response to the tune played. These gestures, together with the top knot and the clothes suggest that this figure might be a wandering holy man of the Vaishnava sect or more likely Vishnu himself as an ascetic.

53

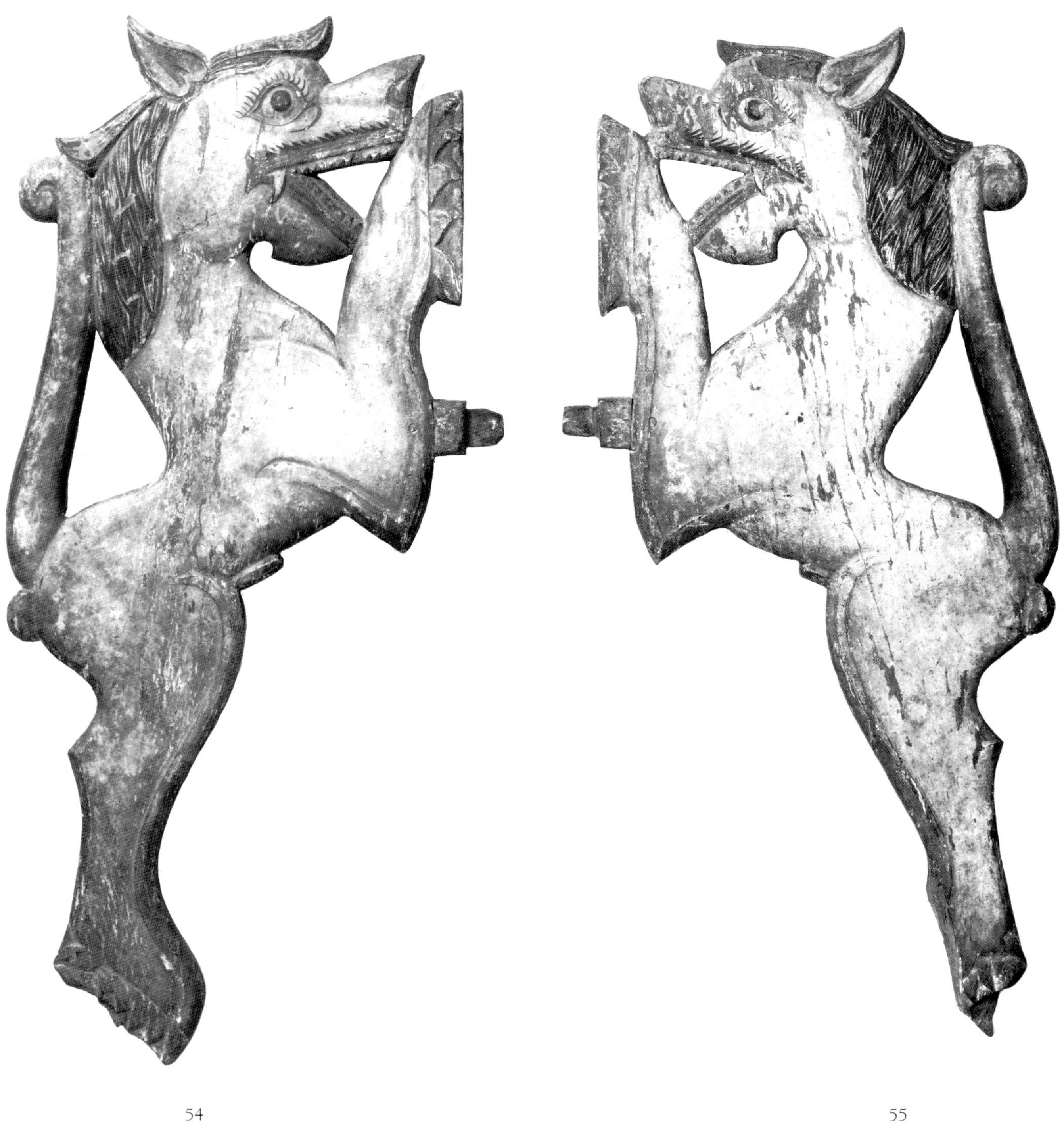

54

55

54–55. Leogryph Brackets

Painted wood/ Height: 27″
Nineteenth-twentieth century
Gift of Saul and Hilda Mehlman, 1985
85.504A & B

These auspicious animals have large expressive faces with huge eyes and bared fangs. These two brackets might have supported a wooden lintel or shelf in a large home shrine.

56–58. *Pot Covers*

Terracotta/ Diameters: 8 ⅜″–10½″
Twentieth century
Gift of Dr. and Mrs. Richard J. Nalin, 1988
88.484, 88.485, 88.487

Such terracotta covers are normally used to seal large rice-storage jars. The images of deities painted on them transform them, however, from domestic utensils to ritual implements. They are used in the worship of Lakshmi, the goddess of wealth and fortune, on special occasions such as the celebration of the rice harvest on the day of the autumnal full moon. These covers are then placed on wooden platforms or at the center of rice-paste patterns on the floor along with various other offerings to the goddess. Subsequently, they are hung on the walls of the home and are auspicious ornaments.[1]

Two of these (nos. 57 and 58) depict images of Durga as Mahishamardini, and the third (no. 56) depicts Krishna embracing Radha. On the lower register of all these covers the earth goddess is represented. She carries sheaves of rice in her hands, recalling the harvest rituals in which these covers are used.[2]

1. Datta (1990), pp. 102–3.
2. See also Bussabarger and Robins (1968), p. 53.

57

58

Malhar men sell dokra ware to Hindu women of the neighboring village.

A craftsman displays votive dokra objects set out on unhusked rice.

Votive Objects and Toys

Votive objects are intended primarily for temporary use in seasonal festivals, in the fulfillment of vows, and for other domestic rites. Certain votive images and vessels can be associated with particular cults. Earthen pots depicting snakes, for instance, are used in the worship of Manasa. Painted pot covers are used to invoke Lakshmi during the harvest season. However, village objects such as clay female figurines and *dokra* animals may be used in many ways. They can take part in the performance of vows, call forth the benevolent forces of nature, or appease demonic ones. A goddess figurine, for instance, could be offered to Manasa for protection against snakebite, to Shitala for protection against smallpox, or to Shashthi for safeguarding infants against premature death. If consecrated, a terracotta figurine can serve a ritual purpose or used simply as household decoration or as a child's toy.

These images are of temporary use. The materials employed, usually clay, wood, or scrap metal, are inexpensive and easily available. The time and effort expended on their production is minimal, and consequently, they may seem stylized or unsophisticated in technique; yet these forms possess a liveliness and spontaneity that distinguish them from more durable metal images in this collection.

59

60

59–63. *Owl, Peacock, Fish, and Mango*

Brass/Metal/ Heights: 4¼″–6½″
Twentieth century
Gift of Dr. David R. Nalin, 1988
88.379, 88.380, 88.381, 88.383

These small *dokra* figurines are made in eastern India, often by low-caste craftsmen such as the Malhar of Dariapur, West Bengal. This "resin-wire" form of *cire perdue* casting has been used to make objects for both tribal and rural use. These objects also appear as votive offerings in urban home shrines from Calcutta to Gujarat. Many of these objects gain significance by their symbolical association with wealth and fertility. Mangoes, for instance, grow abundantly in the summer and are a well-liked food item (no. 63). Nos. 61 and 62 represent two different varieties of fish from the market, no. 62 a remarkably naturalistic representation of a popular and prolific fresh-water fish known as *rohu*, which is cooked and eaten in most parts of Bengal. *Dokra* animals have also become associated with the worship of particular deities. The owl (no. 59), for instance, is a popular votive offering to Lakshmi, the goddess of prosperity (no. 14).[1]

1. See Dallapiccola (1984), p. 74, and Bussabarger and Robins (1968), pp. 92–93.

61

62

63

64–66. *Terracotta Figurines*

Terracotta / Heights: 4¾″–5″
Twentieth century
Gift of Dr. David R. Nalin, 1988
88.338, 88.339, 88.341

These votive figurines are purchased inex-
pensively by village women and carried on
pilgrimages to local temples, placed under
roadside tree shrines, and worshiped in
home shrines on special occasions. They are
probably offered by women to their goddesses as part of fertility rituals.[1]

These figurines, which represent fertility
goddesses, reflect a class of terracottas Stella
Kramrisch has described as "timeless."[2]
Mother goddess figurines with similar typology have been discovered from as early
as the third millennium B.C.E. at sites in the
Indus Valley.

1. Compare Shah (1985), p. 124.
2. Kramrisch (1983), 69.

67. *Elephant and Rider*

Glazed Terracotta / Height: 6″
Twentieth century
Gift of Dr. David R. Nalin, 1988   88.312

This terracotta toy is a twentieth-century
variation based on earlier predecessors. Although the figure of the rider seems stylisti-
cally similar in its "timeless" abstraction to
the previous goddess figurines (nos. 64–66),
the elephant and canopy are quite contemporary.[1] The object has been given a thin
white glaze to create a curio that, in part, can
better serve a contemporary tourist market.
These clay elephants parallel or serve as pro-
totypes for even more elaborate *dokra* elephants with howdahs.

1. Kramrisch (1983), p. 69.

68–72

68–72. *Terracotta Toys*

Painted Terracotta/ Heights: 3½″–4″
Twentieth century
Gift of Dr. David R. Nalin, 1988
88.310, 88.343, 88.344, 88.345, 88.346

These animal figurines are made by village potters, who mold the clay by hand, fire, and then paint them in bright colors, and are often sold to tribals. They can be found widely in weekly rural markets and fairs. They may be seen decaying at roadside shrines, where they are offered by travelers. They also make inexpensive but attractive toys for children. Like the *dokra* figurines, they can be used as simple votive offerings in home shrines. The examples shown here are of two horses, two bulls, and an elephant.[1]

1. See Shah (1985), pp. 174–190.

Bibliography

ART FORMS OF BENGAL

Alpana. New Delhi: Publications Division, Ministry of Information and Broadcasting, Govt. of India, 1976.

Archer, W. G. *Kalighat Paintings.* London: Victoria & Albert Museum, 1971.

Art in Industry Through the Ages. (Monograph series on Bengal) New Delhi: Navrang, 1976.

Asher, Frederick M. *The Art of Eastern India, 300–800.* Minneapolis: University of Minnesota Press, 1980.

Bandopadhyaya, Amiyakumara. *Banglalakshmira Jhampi.* Kalikata: Ananda, 1979.

Bandopadhyay, Bimal. *Metal Sculptures of Eastern India.* Delhi: Sundeep Prakashan, 1981.

Bardhan, Prativabala. *Alimpan.* Calcutta: Reproduction Syndicate, 1968.

Bhaduri, Agnibarna. *Ekalera Silpacinta.* Kalikata: Subarnarekha, 1986.

Bhattacharya, Asok K. "On the Origins of the School of Kalighat Painting." *Journal of the Indian Society of Oriental Art* 15 (1985–86): 53–57.

Bhattasali, Nalinikanta. *Iconography of Buddhist and Brahmanical Sculptures in the Dacca Museum.* Dacca, 1929.

———. "Wooden Sculpture of Ancient Bengal." *Modern Review* XLV: 442–445.

Chatterji, Tapanmohan. *Alpana: Ritual Decoration in Bengal.* Bombay: Orient Longmans, 1948.

Das, Sudhir Ranjan. *Folk Ritual Drawing of Bengal, A Study in Origins.* Calcutta: Calcutta University Press, 1950.

Datta, Sarojit. *Folk Paintings of Bengal.* New Delhi: Khama Publishers, 1993.

Dutt, Guru Saday. *Catalogue of Folk Arts.* Calcutta: Indian Society of Oriental Art, 1932.

———. *Folk Arts and Crafts of Bengal: The Collected Papers.* Calcutta: Seagull, 1990.

———. "The Indigenous Painters of Bengal." *Journal of the Indian Society of Oriental Art* 1 (1933): 17–25.

———. "A Wood Carving From a Bengal Village." *Journal of the Indian Society of Oriental Art* 5 (1937): 29–31.

Gangoly, O. C. "Art of the Pala Empire of Bengal." *Rupam* 37 (1929): 59.

Ganguli, K. K. *Designs in Traditional Arts of Bengal.* Calcutta: Directorate of Industries, 1963.

Ghose, Benoy. *Pascimbangera Samskriti.* Calcutta: Prakash Bhavan, 1994.

———. *Traditional Arts and Crafts of West Bengal: A Sociological Survey.* Calcutta: Papyrus, 1981.

Ghosh, D. P. "An Illustrated Ramayana Manuscript of Tulsidas and Pats from Bengal." *Journal of the Indian Society of Oriental Art* 13 (1945): 129–139.

Gupta, Eva Maria. *Brata und Alpana in Bengalen.* Wiesbaden: Steiner, 1983.

Gupta, Sankar Sen. *The Patas and the Patuas of Bengal.* Calcutta: Indian Publications, 1973.

Handbook of Bengal School. New Delhi: National Gallery of Modern Art, 1975.

Handicrafts Survey Monograph on Dokra Artisans of Dariapur (Burdwan). Government of India, 1973.

Haque, Zulekha. *Terracotta Decorations of Late Medieval Bengal: Portrayal of a Society.* Dacca: Asiatic Society of Bangladesh, 1980.

Horne, Lee. "Brasscasters of Dariapur, West Bengal: Artisans in a Changing World." *Expeditions* 29 (1987): 39–46.

———. "Linking the Past with the Present: Ethnoarchaeology in a Museum Context." *Museum* 157: 57–61.

Huntington, Susan L. *The "Pala-Sena" Schools of Sculpture.* Leiden: E. J. Brill, 1984.

Kar, Cintamani, ed. *Alo Bhubana Bhara.* Kalikata: Iyam Raitarsera, 1389.

Kramrisch, Stella. "Kantha." *Journal of the Indian Society of Oriental Art* 7 (1939): 141–167.

———. "Pala and Sena Sculpture." *Rupam* 40 (1929): 107–126.

Mandala, Satyananda. *Dakshina Cabbisa Paraganara Lokasilpa.* Kalikata, 1391.

Mazumdar, Nirod. *Punasca Pari.* Kalikata: Ananda, 1983.

Mitra, Debala and Gouriswar Bhattacharya, eds. *Studies in Art and Archaeology of Bihar and Bengal: Nalinikanta Satavarsiki Dr. N. K. Bhattasali Centenary Volume.* Delhi: Sri Satguru Publications, 1989.

Mitra, S. K., ed. *East Indian Bronzes.* Calcutta: Calcutta University Press, 1979.

Mookerjee, Ajitcoomar. *Folk Art of Bengal, A Study of an Art for and of, the People.* Calcutta: Calcutta University Press, 1946.

Mortaza, Dewan Golam. *Lokayata Palaparbana: Katha, Kamana, Alpana.* Dhaka: Pratisthana, 1988.

Mukherjee, Meera. *Folk Metal Craft of Eastern India.* Delhi: All India Handicrafts Board, 1977.

———. *Metal Craftsmen of India.* Calcutta: Anthropological Survey of India, 1978.

———. "Metalcraftsmen, Their Work and Environments." *Journal of the Indian Anthropological Society* 19, no. 1 (1984): 66–79.

Mukhopadhyay, Somnath. *Candi in Art and Iconography.* Delhi: Agam, 1984.

Pal, Pratapaditya. *Indian Sculpture.* Vol. 2. Los Angeles: Los Angeles County Museum of Art, 1988.

Ray, N. R. *Eastern Indian Bronzes.* Delhi: Lalit Kala Academy, 1986.

Ray, Sudhansu. *Ritual Art of the Bratas of Bengal.* Calcutta, 1961.

Ray, S. K. "The Artisan Castes of West Bengal and Their Craft." In *The Tribes and Castes of West Bengal: Census of India 1951: West Bengal.* Calcutta: West Bengal Government Press, 1953.

Ray, S. K. "Primitive Statuettes of West Bengal." *Journal of Arts and Crafts* 1, no. 1 (January 1939): 1–8.

Reeves, Ruth. *Cire Perdue Casting in India.* Delhi: Crafts Museum, 1962.

Saraswati, S. K. *Early Sculpture of Bengal.* Calcutta: Sree Saraswaty Press, Ltd., 1962.

Sirajuddin, Muhammad. *Living Crafts in Bangladesh.* Dhaka: Markup International, 1992.

Soma, Shobhana and Anila Acarya, eds. *Bamla Silpa Samalocanara Dhara.* Kalikata: Anushtupa Prakashani, 1986.

Tiger, Rebecca. "Narrative Folk *Pats* of West Bengal: Approaches to the Analysis of Painted Scrolls in Village India." (Unpublished Master's Thesis, University of Pennsylvania, 1975).

EXHIBITION CATALOGUES

Aditi: The Living Arts of India. Washington DC: Smithsonian Institution Press, 1985.

The Arts of Bengal and Eastern India. Calcutta: Crafts Council of West Bengal, 1982.

Aryan, S. *A Catalogue of Indian Folk and Tribal Art in the Collection of Home of Folk Art.* India Offset Printers, 1990.

Basu, Ashish. *Handicrafts of West Bengal—A Retrospect.* Calcutta, 1990.

Bussabarger, Robert F. and Betti Dashew Robins. *The Everyday Art of India.* New York: Dover Publications, 1968.

Casey, Jane Anne, ed. *Medieval Sculpture from Eastern India. Selections from the Nalin Collection.* Livingston, NJ: Nalin International Publications, 1985.

Chakraborti, Siten and Krishnabari Radha. *Handicrafts of West Bengal*. Calcutta: Institute of Art & Handicraft, 1991.

Chattopadhyay, Kamaladevi. *Indian Handicrafts*. New Delhi: Allied Publishers, 1963.

Dallapiccola, A. L., ed. *The Sacred and the Profane: Bell Metal Casting in the Folk Art of India*. Heidelberg: Völkerkundmuseum der von-Portheim-Stiftung, 1984.

Davidson, Leroy J. *Art of the Indian Subcontinent From Los Angeles Collections*. Los Angeles: The Ward Ritchie Press, 1968.

Desai, Vishakha N. and Darielle Mason, eds. *Gods, Guardians, and Lovers*. New York: The Asia Society Galleries, 1993.

Dhamija, Jasleen. *Indian Folk Arts and Crafts*. New Delhi: National Book Trust, 1970.

Fischer, Eberhard, Jyotindra Jain, and Haku Shah. *Tempeltücher für die Muttergöttinen in Indien: Zeremonien, Herstellung und Ikonographie gemalter und gedruckter Stoffbilder aus Gujarat*. Zürich: Museum Rietberg, 1982.

Fisher, Nora, ed. *Mud, Mirror and Thread. Folk Traditions of Rural India*. Ahmedabad: Mapin Publishing Pvt. Ltd. and Santa Fe: Museum of New Mexico Press, 1993.

Hacker, Katherine F. and Krista J. Turnbull. *Courtyard, Bazaar, Temple: Traditions of Textile Expression in India*. Seattle: University of Washington, Costume and Textile Study Center, 1982.

Haas, Suzanne, Marie-Louise Nabholz-Kartaschoff and Marlene Lang-Meyer. *Götter, Tiere, Blümen: Gelbguss und Stickereien aus Indien*. Basel: Museum für Völkerkunde und Schweizerische Museum für Volkskunde, 1987.

In the Image of Man: The Indian Perception of the Universe through 2000 years of Painting and Sculpture. New York: Alpine Fine Arts Collection, Ltd., 1982.

Jain, Jyotindra. *Painted Myths of Creation: Art and Ritual of an Indian Tribe*. New Delhi: Lalit Kala Akademi, 1984.

———, ed. *Utensils*. Ahmedabad: The Gujarat Handicrafts Development Corporation Ltd. and VECHAAR, 1990.

Jain, Jyotindra and Aarti Aggarwala. *National Handicrafts and Handlooms Museum New Delhi*. Ahmedabad: Mapin Publishing Pvt. Ltd., 1989.

Jayakar, Pupul. *The Earthen Drum: An Introduction to the Ritual Arts of Rural India*. New Delhi: National Museum, 1978.

Kalpesi, Roshan. *Shilpakar: The Indian Craftsman*. Bombay: Marg Publications, 1982.

Kramrisch, Stella. *Manifestations of Śiva*. Philadelphia: Philadelphia Museum of Art, 1981.

———. *Unknown India. Ritual Art in Tribe and Village*. Philadelphia: Philadelphia Museum of Art, 1968.

Longenecker, Martha. *India: Village Tribal, Ritual Arts*. San Diego: Mingei International Museum of Folk Art, 1981.

Mahamaya: The Crafts and Craftsmen of Eastern India. Calcutta: The Crafts Council of West Bengal, 1986.

Mallebrein, Cornelia. *Die anderen Götter: Volks- und Stammesbronzen aus Indien*. Heidelberg: Raus, 1993.

Pal, M. K. *Asutosh Museum of Indian Art: An Introduction*. Calcutta: Calcutta University Press, 1962.

Patua Art: Development of the Scroll Paintings of Bengal Commemorating the Bicentenary of the French Revolution. Calcutta: Alliance Française of Calcutta & Crafts Council of West Bengal, 1989.

Poster, Amy. *From Indian Earth: 4000 Years of Terracotta Art*. New York: The Brooklyn Museum, 1986.

Shah, Haku. *Form and Many Forms of Mother Clay*. Delhi: National Crafts Museum, 1985.

Skelton, Robert and Mark Francis. *Arts of Bengal: The Heritage of Bangladesh and Eastern India*. London: The Whitechapel Art Gallery, 1979.

ETHNOGRAPHY

Beech, Mary Higdon. "The Domestic Realm in the Lives of Hindu Women in Calcutta." In *Separate Worlds: Studies of Purdah in South Asia*, edited by Hanna Papanek and Gail Minault, 110–135. Delhi: Chanakya Publications, 1982.

Bhattacharyya, Anjali. "Mothers, Daughters and the Changing Rural Scene." In *Shaping Bengali Worlds*, edited by Tony K. Stewart, 190–196. East Lansing, MI: Asian Studies Center, Michigan State University, 1989.

Bhattacharyya, Manibrata. "Purity and Impurity in the Death Rituals of Bengal." In *Bengal: Studies in Literature, Society and History*, edited by Marvin Davis, 115–120. East Lansing, MI: Asian Studies Center, Michigan State University, 1976.

Corwin, Lauren Anita. "Female Roles: Change Over Time in Middle Class Calcutta." In *Shaping Bengali Worlds*, edited by Tony K. Stewart, 181–190. East Lansing, MI: Michigan State University, 1989.

Dalton, E. T. *Descriptive Ethnology of Bengal*. Calcutta: Thacker, Spink & Co., 1872.

Dimock, Edward C., Jr. "Manasa, Goddess of Snakes: The Sasthi Myth." In *Myths and Symbols. Studies in Honor of Mircea Eliade*, edited by Joseph M. Kitagawa, and Charles H. Long, 217–226. Chicago: University of Chicago Press, 1969.

———. *The Sound of Silent Guns and Other Essays*. Delhi: Oxford University Press, 1989.

——— ed., *Studies in Bengali Literature, History, and Society*. New York: Learning Resources in International Studies, 1974.

———. "A Theology of the Repulsive: The Myth of the Goddess Sitala." In *The Divine Consort: Radha and the Goddesses of India*, edited by John Stratton Hawley and Donna Marie Wulff, 184–203. Boston: Beacon Press, 1982.

Fruzetti, Lina. *The Gift of a Virgin: Women, Marriage and Ritual in a Bengali Society*. New Brunswick, NJ: Rutgers University Press, 1982.

Fruzzetti, Lina, and Akos Ostor. *Kinship and Ritual in Bengal*. New Delhi: South Asian Publishers, 1984.

Hunter, William Wilson. *Annals of Rural Bengal*. London: Smith, Elder, and Co., 1897.

Inden, Ronald B. and Ralph W. Nicholas. *Kinship in Bengali Culture*. Chicago: University of Chicago Press, 1977.

Kennedy, Melville T. *The Chaitanya Movement*. New York: Garland Publishing, Inc., 1981.

Mazumdar, Shudha. *A Pattern of Life: The Memoirs of an Indian Women*. Delhi: Manohar, 1977.

McCutchion, David. "The Temples of Calcutta." *Journal of the Indian Society of Oriental Art* 87 (1968): 45–58.

Mitra, A. *Fairs and Festivals in West Bengal*. Calcutta: West Bengal Government Press, 1953.

Mookerjee, Ajit. *Kali: The Feminine Force*. New York: Destiny Books, 1988.

Nicholas, Ralph W. "The Bengali Calendar and the Hindu Religious Year in Bengal." In *The Study of Bengal: New Contributions to the Humanities and Social Sciences*, edited by Peter J. Bertocci, 17–29. East Lansing, MI: Asian Studies Center, Michigan State University, 1982.

———. "Ritual Hierarchy and Social Relations in Rural Bengal." In *Contributions to Indian Sociology* 1 (1967): 56–83.

———. "The Village Mother in Bengal." In *Mother Worship*, edited by James D. Preston, 192–201. Chapel Hill, NC: University of North Carolina Press, 1982.

O'Connell, Joseph T., ed. *Bengal Vaisnavism, Orientalism, Society and the Arts*. East Lansing, MI: Asian Studies Center, Michigan State University, 1985.

Ostor, Akos. *The Play of the Gods: Locality, Ideology, Structure, and the Festivals of a Bengali Town*. Chicago: University of Chicago Press, 1980.

Ostor, Akos, Lina Fruzzetti and Steve Barnett. "The Cultural Construction of the Person in Bengal and Tamil Nadu." In *Concepts of Person: Kinship, Caste and Marriage in India*, 8–30. Cambridge, MA: Harvard University Press, 1980.

Paul, Robert, and Mary Jane Beech, eds. *Bengal: Change and Continuity*. East Lansing, MI: Asian Studies Center, Michigan State University, 1969.

Robinson, J. D. "Village Tradition and Historical Sources in West Bengal." In *The Cultural Heritage of the Indian Village*, edited by Brian Durrans and T. Richard Blurton, 135–140. London: British Museum, 1991.

Roy, Manisha. *Bengali Women*. Chicago: University of Chicago Press, 1975.

Sen, Sukumar. *Women's Dialect in Bengali*. Calcutta: Jijnasa, 1979.

Sen Gupta, Sankar. *A Study of Women of Bengal*. Calcutta: Indian Publications, 1970.

Stewart, Tony K., ed. *Shaping Bengali Worlds, Public and Private*. East Lansing, MI: Asian Studies Center, Michigan State University, 1989.

Suhasini Debi. *Meyeli Bratakatha*. Kalikata: Pustaka Bipani, 1392.

Tagore, Abanindranath. *Banglar Brata*. Calcutta: Visvabharati, 1943.

Wander, Nathaniel. "Fire and Water in the Enactment of Caste Ideology in West Bengal." In *Research on Bengal: Proceedings of the 1981 Bengal Studies Conference*, edited by Ray Langsten, 35–44. East Lansing, MI: Asian Studies Center, Michigan State University, 1983.

MISCELLANEOUS

Achaya, K. T. *Indian Food: A Historical Companion*. Delhi: Oxford University Press, 1994.

Appadurai, Arjun. "Introduction: Commodities and the Politics of Value." In *The Social Life of Things: Commodities in Cultural Perspective*, edited by Arjun Appadurai, 3–63. Cambridge: Cambridge University Press, 1986.

Archer, Mildred. *Indian Popular Painting in the India Office Library*. New Delhi: UBS Publishers' Distributors Ltd, 1977.

Babb, Lawrence A. *The Divine Hierarchy: Popular Hinduism in Central India*. New York: Columbia University Press, 1975.

Banerjea, J. N. *The Development of Hindu Iconography*. Calcutta: Calcutta University Press, 1956.

Bhardwaj, Surinder Mohan. *Hindu Places of Pilgrimage in India: A Cultural Geography*. Berkeley: University of California Press, 1973.

Bhushan, Jamila Brij. *Indian Jewellery, Ornaments and Decorative Designs*. Bombay: D. B. Taraporevala Sons & Co., 1964.

Blackburn, Stuart. "Death and Deification: Folk Cults in Hinduism." *History of Religions* 24, no. 3 (February 1985): 255–75.

Breckenridge, Carol A. "The Social Use of Everyday Objects in Hindu South India." In *Dimensions of Indian Art. Pupul Jayakar Seventy*, edited by Lokesh Chandra and Jyotindra Jain, 57–66. New Delhi: Agam Prakash, 1986.

Chatterjee, Ashoke. "Challenges of Transition: Design and Craft in India." In *Making Things in South Asia: The Role of Artist and Craftsman* (Proceedings of the South Asia Seminar 4), edited by Michael W. Meister, 3–9. Philadelphia: Department of South Asia Regional Studies, 1988.

Coomaraswamy, Ananda K. *The Indian Craftsman*. London: Probsthain and Co., 1909.

———. "The Nature of 'Folklore' and 'Popular Art'." *Indian Art and Letters*, XI, no. 2 (1937): 76–84.

———. "What Is the Use of Art, Anyway?" In *Why Exhibit Works of Art?* London: Luzac & Co., 1943.

Cort, Louise Allison. "The Role of the Potter in South Asia." In *Making Things in South Asia: The Role of Artist and Craftsman* (Proceedings of the South Asia Seminar 4), edited by Michael W. Meister, 165–74. Philadelphia: Department of South Asia Regional Studies, 1988.

———. "Temple Potters of Puri." *RES.* 8 (1984): 33–43.

Das, Veena. "On the Categorization of Space in Hindu Ritual." In *Text and Context: The Social Anthropology of Tradition*, edited by Ravindra Jain, 9–27. Philadelphia: Institute for Study of Human Issues, 1977.

Davis, Richard. *Ritual in an Oscillating Universe*. Princeton: Princeton University Press, 1991.

Davis, Richard. "Loss and Recovery of Ritual Self Among Hindu Images." *Journal of Ritual Studies* 6, no. 1 (Winter 1992): 43–62.

Doshi, Saryu, ed. *Tribal India. Ancestors, Gods and Spirits*. Bombay: Marg Publications, 1992.

Doshi, Saryu. "Traditional Ornaments: Fluctuations in Taste." In *Symbols and Manifestations of Indian Art*, edited by Saryu Doshi, 65–76. Bombay: Marg Publications, 1984.

Dube S. C., ed. *Tribal Heritage of India*. New Delhi: Vikas Publishing House, 1977.

Eaton, Richard M. *The Rise of Islam and the Bengal Frontier, 1204–1760*. Berkeley: University of California Press, 1993.

Eck, Diana. *Darsan: Seeing the Divine Image in India*. Chambersburg, PA: Anima Books, 1985.

Eck, Diana. "Ganga: The Goddess in Hindu Sacred Geography." In *The Division Consort: Radha and the Goddesses of India*, edited by John Stratton Hawley and Donna Marie Wulff, 166–183. Boston: Beacon Press, 1982.

Eliade, Mircea. *The Sacred and the Profane: The Nature of Religion*. New York: Harcourt, Brace & Jovanovich, 1959.

Eschmann, Anncharlott, Hermann Kulke, and Gaya Charan Tripathi. *The Cult of Jagannath and the Regional Tradition of Orissa*. Delhi: Manohar, 1978.

Fuller, C. J. *The Camphor Flame: Popular Hinduism and Society in India*. Princeton: Princeton University Press, 1992.

Gonda, Jan. *Eye and Gaze in the Veda*. Amsterdam: North Holland Publishing Company, 1969.

Hacker, Katherine F. "Continuities and Transformations Among Living Sculptural Traditions: Wax-Thread Metal Images of Eastern India." (Ph. D. Diss., University of Pennsylvania, 1993).

Hanchett, Suzanne. *Coloured Rice: Symbolic Structure in Hindu Family Festivals*. Delhi: Hindustan Publishing Corporation, 1988.

Huyler, Stephen P. *Village India*. New York, 1985.

Inglis, Stephen. "Making and Breaking: Craft Communities in South Asia." In *Making Things in South Asia: The Role of the Artist and Craftsman* (Proceedings of the South Asia Seminar 4), edited by Michael W. Meister, 153–64. Philadelphia: Department of South Asia Regional Studies, 1988.

———. "Possession and Pottery: Serving the Divine in a South Indian Community." In *Gods of Flesh/Gods of Stone: The Embodiment of Divinity in India*, edited by Joanne Punzo Waghorne and Norman Cutler, 89–102. Chambersburg, PA: Anima Books, 1985.

Jain-Neubauer, Jutta, and Jyotindra Jain. "Wall Decorations of a Mobile People." In *The Impulse to Adorn: Studies in Traditional Indian Architecture*, edited by Jan Pieper and George Michell, 33–42. Bombay: Marg Publications, 1982.

Khare, R. S. *Culture and Reality*. Simla: Indian Institute of Advanced Study, 1976.

Khare, R. S., ed. *Aspects in South Asian Food Systems: Food, Society and Culture*. Durham: Carolina Academic Press, 1986.

Kinsley, David R. *Hindu Goddesses: Visions of the Divine Feminine in the Hindu Religious Tradition*. Berkeley: University of California Press, 1986.

———. "The Portrait of the Goddess in the Devi-Mahatmya." *Journal of the American Academy of Religion* 46, no. 4 (December 1978): 489–506.

Kramrisch, Stella. "Indian Terracottas." In *Exploring India's Sacred Art: Selected Writings of Stella Kramrisch*, edited by Barbara Stoler Miller, 69–83. Philadelphia: University of Pennsylvania Press, 1983.

———. "Indian Varieties of Art Rituals." In *Myths and Symbols: Studies in Honor of Mircea Eliade*, edited by Joseph M. Kitagawa and Charles H. Long, 23–46. Chicago and London: University of Chicago Press, 1969.

Majumdar, R. C. *The History of Bengal*. Vol. I: Hindu Period. Dacca: University of Dacca Press, 1943.

Meister, Michael W., ed. *Making Things in South Asia: The Role of Artist and Craftsman*. Philadelphia: Department of South Asia Regional Studies, 1988.

Mishra, Umesh Chandra. *Tribal Paintings and Sculptures*. Delhi: B. R. Publishing Corp., 1989.

Mitter, Partha. *Much Maligned Monsters: A History of European Reactions to Indian Art*. Oxford: Clarendon Press, 1977.

Mode, Heinz and Subodh Chandra. *Indian Folk Art*. New York: Alpine Fine Arts Collection, Ltd., 1985.

Monier-Williams, Sir Monier. *Sanskrit-English Dictionary*. New Delhi: Munshiram Manoharlal Publishers, 1976.

Moore, Melinda A. "The Kerala House as a Hindu Cosmos." *Contributions to Indian Sociology* 23 (1989): 169–202.

O'Flaherty, Wendy Doniger. "The Role of Myth in the Indian Life Cycle." In *Aditi: The Living Arts of India*, 185–201. Washington DC: The Smithsonian Institution, 1986.

Pal, M. K. *Crafts and Craftsmen in Traditional India*. New Delhi: Kanak Publications, 1978.

Prakash, Swatantra. "The Living Arts of India: Craftsmen at Work." In *Pageant of Indian Art. Festival of India in Great Britain*, edited by Saryu Doshi, 125–32. Bombay: Marg Publications, 1983.

Pramar, V. S. "Sociology of the North Gujarat Urban House." *Contributions to Indian Sociology* 21 (1987): 331–346.

Raheja, Gloria G. *The Poison in the Gift*. Chicago: University of Chicago Press, 1988.

Rao, T. A. G. *Elements of Hindu Iconography*. New York: Paragon Oriental Series, 1968.

Saraf, D. N. *Indian Crafts: Development and Potential*. New Delhi: Vikas Publishing House, 1982.

Saraswathi, B. "Caste, Craft and Change." *Man in India* 43, no. 3 (July/Sept. 1963): 218–24.

Sarkar, Jadu-Nath. *The History of Bengal*. Vol. II: Muslim Period, 1200–1757. Dacca: University of Dacca Press, 1948.

Sen, Dinesh Chandra. *Bengali Language and Literature*. Calcutta: Calcutta University Press, 1911.

———. *The Vaisnava Literature of Medieval Bengal*. Calcutta: Calcutta University Press, 1917.

Singer, Milton. "Changing Craft Traditions in India." In *Labor Commitment and Social Change in Developing Areas,* edited by Wilbert E. Moore and Arnold Feldman, 258–76. New York: Social Science Research Council, 1960.

Singh G. R. and David C. Scott. "Invoked Spirit Possession Among Some Tribals in Mid-India." *India Cultures Quarterly* 30 (1975): 35–80.

Sircar, D. C., ed. *The Sakta Pithas*. Delhi: Motilal Banarsidass, 1973.

———. *The Sakti Cult and Tara*. Calcutta: Calcutta University Press, 1967.

Soundara Rajan, K. V. *Indian Religious Art: Ideas and Ideals*. Delhi, 1983.

Vidhyarthi, L. P. "Cultural Change Among the Tribals of India." In *Rise of Anthropology in India: A Social Science Orientation*. Vol. 1: The Tribal Dimensions, 434–59. Delhi, 1978.

Wadley, Susan, S. *Shakti: Power in the Conceptual Structure of Karimpur Religion*. Chicago: University of Chicago Press, 1975.

———, ed. *The Powers of Tamil Women*. Syracuse: Syracuse University Press, 1980.

Waghorne, Joanne Punzo. "Dressing the Body of God: South Indian Bronze Sculpture in Its Temple Setting." *Asian Art Journal* (Summer 1992): 9–33.

Waghorne, Joanne Punzo and Norman Cutler, eds. *Gods of Flesh/Gods of Stone: The Embodiment of Divinity in India*. Chambersburg, PA: Anima Books, 1985.

Williams, Joanna G. "Criticizing and Evaluating the Visual Arts in India: A Preliminary Example." *The Journal of Asian Studies* 47, no. 1 (February 1988): 3–28.

———. "From the Fifth to the Twentieth Century and Back." *Art Journal* 49, no. 4 (Winter 1990): 363–69.

———. "Siva and the Cult of Jagannath: Iconography and Ambiguity." In *Discourses on Śiva: Proceedings of a Symposium on the Nature of Religious Imagery,* edited by Michael W. Meister, 298–311. Philadelphia: University of Pennsylvania Press, 1984.

Zimmer, Heinrich. *Myths and Symbols in Indian Art*. Princeton, NJ: Bollingen Foundation, 1974.